2020 DOLLYWOOD AND BEYOND!

MICHAEL FRIDGEN

Copyright © 2020 by Michael Fridgen

All rights reserved.

ISBN 13: 978-0-9968574-6-8

Dreamlly Books: Minneapolis, Minnesota

For Dad and Mom

Like all guidebooks, the information in this guide is subject to change without notice. Theme parks, hotels, and restaurants are dynamic places and the author does not take responsibility for changes that occur after printing. Also, traffic patterns and road construction can change with each season. Always check for updated information on dollywood.com before departure. All maps in this guide are for reference and meant to offer a point of orientation. The maps in this guide are not drawn to scale and are original work of the author.

The author of this book is in no way connected to Dollywood, Dollywood's Splash Country, Dollywood's DreamMore Resort, Dolly Parton, Herschend Family Entertainment, the Dollywood Company or any other travel enterprise located in Tennessee. The information and opinions expressed in this guide belong to the author and do not represent, in any way, the beliefs of Herschend Family Entertainment, Dolly Parton, or any of their enterprises.

Special acknowledgement is given to Donald Lewis for testing the descriptions in this guide. The photographs on this book's cover belong to the author.

TABLE OF CONTENTS

CHAPTER 1: INTRODUCTION TO DOLLYWOOD 9
    What is Dollywood? 9
    Consider the Source 11
    All I Really Needed to Know I Learned in Theme Parks 15
    Dollywood History 16
    Great Smoky Mountain Fire of 2016 26

CHAPTER 2: ESSENTIALS 31
    Getting There 31
    Getting Around the Area 34
    Best Time to Visit 36
    Where to Stay 40
    Tickets 58
    What to Pack 65
    Who the Heck Is this Dolly Parton Anyway? 68

CHAPTER 3: DOLLYWOOD 75
    Arrival and Parking 75
    Doggywood 78
    Guest Services 79
    Centralized Measuring and Ride Accessibility Center 83
    TimeSaver Reservation Center 91
    Adventures in Imagination 98
    Jukebox Junction 103
    Rivertown Junction 110
    Country Fair 119
    The Village 124

Owens Farm 130
Craftsman's Valley 133
Wilderness Pass 148
Wildwood Grove.. 156
Timber Canyon 162

CHAPTER 4: DOLLYWOOD'S SPLASH COUNTRY 171
Arrival and Parking...171
Special Rules and Considerations 173
TimeSaver 176
Retreats and Canopies 177
Attractions at Dollywood's Splash Country 179
Food, Snacks, and Beverages 186
Shops 189

CHAPTER 5: EVENTS AND FESTIVALS 191
Dollywood's Festival of Nations 192
Flower and Food Festival.. 193
Barbeque and Bluegrass 194
Summer Celebration..194
Harvest Festival 197
Great Pumpkin LumiNights...199
Smoky Mountain Christmas 200

CHAPTER 6: OUTSIDE DOLLY'S WORLD 207
Dolly Parton's Stampede..207
Pirates Voyage Dinner & Show..211
Sevierville 213
Pigeon Forge 215
The Island.. 218
Gatlinburg 221
Great Smoky Mountains National Park 224
Time to go...228

MAPS
- Map 1: Smoky Mountain Tourist Region 229
- Map 2: Arriving at Dollywood................................230
- Map 3: Dollywood Parking Lots 231
- Map 4: Dollywood Lands....................................... 232

INDEX..**233**

CHAPTER 1

INTRODUCTION TO DOLLYWOOD

WHAT IS DOLLYWOOD?

Much like sweetbread and narwhals, Dollywood is misunderstood. Due to its location and association with country music, most people believe the park to be a type of redneck Disneyland. But as with its namesake and co-owner, Dolly Parton, further examination will prove that Dollywood is much more than its stereotype.

Dollywood is not entirely an amusement park, although it has plenty of thrill rides. It's also not entirely a theme park, although it has strongly themed lands. Dollywood is a rare combination of both, offering the storytelling of Disney along with the roller coasters of a Six Flags. It's a park that grinds its own flour and sends guests dangling 210 feet over the edge of America's first winged coaster. In the same day visitors can ride the fastest wooden roller coaster on the planet and watch a blacksmith pound a hunk of metal into a dinner bell. Between theme and amusement, between the Deep South and New York, between traditional and modern—the park is indefinable. There's no place else like it; it's simply Dollywood!

Two parks, Dollywood and Dollywood's Splash Country, comprise the property. A massive hotel complex, Dollywood's DreamMore Resort, sits adjacent to the theme parks (more about the resort can be found in Chapter 2). Located at the foothills of the Great Smoky Mountains in Pigeon Forge, Tennessee, Dollywood is within a day's drive from one-third of the population of the United States. Approximately 3.5 million visitors pass through Dolly's gates every year. However, a recent and aggressive expansion plan has park officials hoping to attract as many as 5 million annual visitors.

The Dollywood parks are the most visited paid attraction in Tennessee—that's saying something in a state that also includes Graceland, The Grand Ole Opry, and one of the largest universities in the nation. Nashville had its own country music theme park, Opryland, which closed in 1997 due to the site's limited ability to grow. Dollywood seems to have learned from Opryland's demise and is both proactive and strategic in designing future attractions to meet a changing population. You only need to look at the massive loops of the Wild Eagle roller coaster as they gracefully curve over the hills to understand what I mean. But don't make the mistake of thinking that nonriders have been forgotten; a recent season not only introduced a launch-coaster, but also a covered pavilion with plenty of rocking chairs.

With all this said, perhaps the real appeal of Dollywood is its ability to appeal. This may be an awkward sentence, but it's a true statement. When you visit, take some time to sit on a bench and look around at the people passing before you. I am not sure there is any other theme park that attracts as diverse an audience as Dollywood does. Camouflage T-shirts with cargo shorts walk past, as do the bedazzled jeans of suburban moms. The matching shirts of a church youth group are followed by a group of gay guys from Miami. Families with small children walk near a couple of teenagers who have been allowed to explore on their own for the first time. A middle-aged couple is experiencing a trip-of-a-lifetime right next to well-traveled Europeans who want to see more of America than just its two coasts. All have traveled to get a glimpse of Dolly's world. Much like how Walt Disney's legend permeates the Magic Kingdom, Dolly Parton's welcoming spirit fills these hills—and not even the most politically opinionated dare interrupt that infectious spirit. From infants to elderly, singles to families, country folk to urban hipsters...Dollywood has something for everyone.

CONSIDER THE SOURCE

In this age of Wikipedia and corporate publishing it is important to carefully consider the author's expertise, especially while reading a book about travel. Teams of people assigned through a publisher write many bestselling guides and tour books. Sometimes, these writers have not even visited the place they are offering advice about! So, if you're wondering who wrote this book and why you should read it, I'm about to tell you. If you are not wondering, or are anxious to get to the details, go ahead and skip to the next section.

When I was five years old I received a map of Disney World's Magic Kingdom for Christmas. Today, if a kid gets a map of Disney World as a present, they can probably assume that the real gift is an actual trip to the famous park. But I knew that my family did not have the means to make such a journey. I also knew that my parents realized how much I loved looking at maps. Regardless, I can credit my many hours of staring at that map, and using it to drive my Matchbox cars on, as the beginning of my love of theme parks.

I liked maps of real places, too, but these were usually messy with mountains, rivers and lakes to navigate. The Magic Kingdom map was beautifully drawn and instantly made sense to me. I took my little car and easily planned how to get from the entrance gate to the moat around Cinderella Castle. Many nights I dreamed that someday I would spend one day at that magical place. But back then, I had no idea how my life would develop and I couldn't imagine the numerous theme park visits I would one day attain. (Shameless plug: for more information about my love of all things Disney, read my bestselling book *World Traveler's Guide to Disney: How to Visit Mickey's Kingdoms around the Globe*—available at Amazon.com.)

I grew up in Minnesota and every year we took the two-hour journey by station wagon to spend one day at what I thought was the happiest place on earth, Valleyfair in Shakopee, Minnesota. I vividly remember getting little sleep the night before because of all the anticipation. I also remember saying a prayer because I was afraid that if our house burned down during the night we wouldn't be able to go to Valleyfair.

They called Valleyfair a theme park, but even today I'm unsure what the theme was. Back then, a large patriotic man called Colonel John Phillips Oom-pa-pa roamed the asphalt with his girlfriend Chocolate Moose. She was a furry brown moose that wore a frilly dress and straw hat; I always thought she looked like Minnie Pearl from the television show Hee Haw. Valleyfair had these ladybugs that went around in a circle and an enormous green chair where the Jolly Green Giant supposedly sat, although we never saw him.

I'm unsure how that one glorious day each summer, and my Disney World map, turned into a life-long obsession with theme parks. I'd probably need to employ a psychiatrist with deep analytical skills to determine what from my childhood made me crave the fantasy realness of a themed land. But, when it comes down to it, I guess I don't care why or how I got this way because it's a good way to be. Hey, there are a lot of other worse obsessions I could have!

I believe that theme parks are truly magical places because they force us to forget the real world and pause for reflection. Each year, it's where us kids measured our progress toward adulthood. Nothing marks time better than the ride attendant holding up a painted wood pole next to you and stating that you can go on the High Roller. That pole measured both our physical growth and inner bravery. Every summer, our parents saw the changes in us and we saw the difference in ourselves. I didn't grow up in the age of box socials and cotillions. Our annual trip to Valleyfair is how we generation X'ers marked time.

Through some smart decisions and hard work, I've obtained a life where I am fortunate enough to be able to travel to the places I love. I've been to many theme parks in the United States and abroad. I've been multiple times to each of the Disney parks around the globe. I count among my favorite places Ocean Park in Hong Kong, Tivoli Gardens in Copenhagen, and DisneySea in Tokyo. But this book is not about them.

Growing up in America, of course I'd heard of Dolly Parton. But I was almost twenty-years-old before I learned of her theme park. I was a junior in college when we drove from Minnesota to Orlando for my first visit to Disney World. My lifelong dream to see the place from the map on my childhood floor came true! I had a wonderful experience at the most magical place on Earth and thought I'd seen it all. Then, something unexpected occurred on our drive back to Minnesota. We stopped in Knoxville to spend the night and I got some brochures from a rack in the lobby. (Seriously, you could give me a ticket to the Super Bowl and I'd still rather spend time with a good quality hotel brochure rack.)

My first Dollywood brochure and map advertised the opening of the Jukebox Junction land of the park. On the front, Dolly Parton, sporting a poodle-skirt and tight sweater, stood next to a vintage car. I could tell this was no small local amusement park. It was clear from the brochure that Dolly had an actual theme park with immersive themed lands. I was dying to get there!

So, we drove back to Minnesota and as was customary, saved our pennies for another year and another road trip. There was no doubt to any of my family that I would dictate Dollywood as the destination that next summer. (Years before, they gave up trying to convince me with their own vacation ideas and that has made life easier for us all.)

I was hooked the first moment I sat on the Dollywood parking tram and heard a steam locomotive bellow somewhere behind the magical trees that separated the real world from Dolly's. We spent a day in the park and I soaked in as much atmosphere as I could. I didn't have many resources back then and believed this would probably be my only visit to Dollywood. If I'd only known I'd grow up and write a book about it, I would have kept some notes!

But throughout all these years and countless miles traveled, I haven't returned to any other theme park as many times as I've been to Dollywood. In fact, I can't even recall exactly how many times I've passed through the Butterfly Emporium.

All of us take many roles in life. In order for any one place to be considered a true lifelong destination, it must be able to appeal to you during all those changing roles. Dollywood has not disappointed me in this regard. As my own life has changed I've experienced the park in new and different ways.

I have been to Dollywood as:
- a college student traveling with family.
- a working adult traveling with family.
- an uncle with a ten-month-old nephew.
- a grandson with elderly grandparents.
- a single person who just wanted to get away.
- an adult traveling with other adult friends that I coerced into going.
- an uncle with preteen and toddler nephews.
- part of a couple on our honeymoon.
- a person in a wheelchair after having ankle surgery.
- an uncle with a teenage nephew, preteen nephew, and a third kid, my niece.
- part of a couple still choosing to spend vacation time in Tennessee.

In the 1970s, my Grandma chased after me at Valleyfair when I wanted to ride the little boats instead of eating. Thirty years later, I ran around Dollywood trying to find which mountain craft shop she had gone to. I hope in thirty more years my nephews and niece will be able to push me around the theaters as I now push them around the play areas.

And that brings me back to my original point: theme parks are magical places because they give us a pause to mark the progress we make as people. It's my hope that you will travel to Dollywood, or some other park, and use the fantasy realness to mark your own life. Mostly, I hope you've learned from this section that you can trust me to write this guidebook.

ALL I REALLY NEEDED TO KNOW I LEARNED IN THEME PARKS

- A good map is essential to find your way.
- If you want to eat dinner, you can't spend all of your money on games.
- Waiting in line is dull, but it gets better if you can occupy your own brain for a while.
- Respecting other people's space is a good thing to do.
- Facing a fear can be extremely difficult, but the reward is amazing.
- You might be disappointed at times. Just deal with it.
- Like the weather, things will happen that you can't control. Just deal with it.
- Planning ahead makes your day a lot easier.
- Keep track of your stuff because nobody else will.
- Prioritize what you want to do and make choices that lead in that direction.
- Taking care of your body is important if you want to fit on all the rides.
- If your group splits up, always make a plan to find each other again.
- Cleanliness is a good thing, and if you keep things clean, others will too.
- An active fantasy life inspires you to make your real life even better.
- Creativity still means something on this planet.

- A healthy human always has something to look forward to.
- Be nice to all those who are doing their jobs because tomorrow that will be you.
- As you get older, sitting on a bench and watching a roller coaster can be as much fun as riding it yourself.
- Laughter and having fun are an essential part of life worthy of your time and money.

DOLLYWOOD HISTORY

What do Rudolph the Red-Nosed Reindeer, 1954 Hurricane Hazel, and the Cleveland Browns football team have in common? Well, they all played unlikely and important roles in the early formation of what would become the themed mecca of the Smoky Mountains. Let's start at the beginning.

Since no attraction in eastern Tennessee could survive without the influx of visitors brought by the national park, the history of Dollywood begins with the charter of the Great Smoky Mountains National Park in 1934. President Franklin Delano Roosevelt officially dedicated the park in 1940, and it soon became the most visited of all the parks in our venerable United States National Park System. (More information about the national park can be found in chapter 6.)

Nothing good comes without sacrifice and it's wise to pay homage to the thousands of people that gave up much so that we can enjoy this amazing national park. When the park was created in 1934, there were thousands of people living in the hills. The Cherokee, the original settlers of the Smoky Mountains, had mostly moved or perished during the infamous 'Trail of Tears' in 1838. Forty years later the area was settled by immigrants—many of Irish and Welsh decent. These immigrants built homes, barns, schools, and entire villages. By 1920, people began to realize that the incredible beauty of the mountains was beginning to deteriorate due to a growing population.

A national park is an area of intense beauty that is set aside—it belongs to all of us. Consequently, it isn't possible for people to live and work on these protected lands. After receiving a meager compensation from the Depression-era Government, thousands of families relocated elsewhere. Without the sacrifice of the Cherokee and the immigrants who followed them, we would not have the vast unspoiled majesty that is Great Smoky Mountains National Park.

The next important event doesn't happen for nine years, as the country was preoccupied with other things in the early 1940s. (There were some scuffles in Europe and the Pacific that you may have heard about.) Then, in December of 1949, country singer Gene Autry recorded the first and quintessential version of "Rudolph the Red-Nosed Reindeer." It soared to number one on the Billboard Pop Music chart and stayed there over the holiday week. Becoming the first number one song of the new decade, Autry sold several million copies and made a boatload (er...sleighload) of money. Seriously, always remember that of all the great songs of the 1950s, the first number one hit was "Rudolph the Red-Nosed Reindeer!"

Back on the East Coast, in 1950, a group of investors purchased a retired 1917 coal-fired locomotive from the East Tennessee and Western North Carolina Railroad. The narrow gauge engine was retired from its sixty-six-mile route earlier that year. This group of railroad enthusiasts moved the massive piece of history to northern Virginia and began using it for a small tourist railroad in 1952. However, their plans would soon change abruptly.

In 1954 a massive category four storm, Hurricane Hazel, hit the Mid-Atlantic coast of the United States. The storm had already killed over one thousand in Haiti and struck the United States from North Carolina to New Jersey. Causing unprecedented death and damage, the hurricane moved ashore over Pennsylvania and combined with a cold front. The result barreled toward Toronto, and even though it had traveled 680 miles inland, Hazel still produced the winds of a category one storm. Toronto was devastated and the name Hazel was retired from use for North Atlantic hurricanes.

Sadly, Toronto was not the only victim of Hazel's wrath; the small tourist railroad of northern Virginia was located in a floodplain. With the tracks completely washed out, the investors cut their losses and put their prized 1917 locomotive up for sale.

Now, enter Rudolph the Red-Nosed Reindeer and all that money he made for singer Gene Autry. Autry, by now earning a name as an actor in Hollywood, purchased the locomotive and made plans to move it to Hollywood for use in various films and television shows. However, for a reason not known, after two years Gene Autry abandoned his plans for the engine and put it back up for sale in 1956.

Grover Robbins, a North Carolina man with a big idea, purchased the locomotive. Robbins brought the steam engine back to North Carolina and constructed a three-mile loop of track in Blowing Rock. Noting the 1955 success of Walt Disney's fantasy realness in Anaheim, Robbins added a western village around his track and created one of the country's first theme parks, Tweetsie Railroad. It was 1957, before Twitter owned the word 'tweet,' and Robbins named the park after a sound the engine's whistle was known for making.

Due to the popularity of Western films coming out of Hollywood, Tweetsie Railroad became a tourist destination and further additions were made to the park. The train began to stop throughout its route for a staged robbery. Robbins enjoyed the success of his venture and looked for further ways to expand.

When the US Army wanted to sell a steam locomotive used during World War II in Alaska, Robbins acted quickly. He purchased the engine and made arrangements to bring it to the East Coast. However, he didn't need a second engine for Tweetsie Railroad and wished to reach a new audience. Grover purchased some acreage in the foothills of the Smoky Mountains near Pigeon Forge, Tennessee. He hoped the swarms of visitors heading toward the national park and its growing hiking trails would want something else to do while on vacation.

He recreated the track and village of Tweetsie Railroad and made one change. Instead of a staged robbery, this new park would commemorate the centennial of the Civil War with the train being attacked by Union soldiers. Confederate soldiers would eventually defend the railroad during each of its three-mile journeys. Rebel Railroad, Grover Robbins's second park, operated as successfully as Tweetsie Railroad until he died in 1970. Tweetsie Railroad continues to operate under that name in Blowing Rock, North Carolina, to this day.

Upon his death, Tennessee's Rebel Railroad and its venerable World War II locomotive were for sale. The park and train were quickly purchased that same year by entrepreneur and savvy-investor Art Modell. Modell also owned the Cleveland Browns football team during this time. Being a Yankee, Modell removed the Civil War theme and renamed the park Goldrush Junction.

Goldrush Junction continued to succeed as the family roadtrip vacation became increasingly popular during the 1970s. Several additional structures were added to the park, including a beautiful chapel tucked back in the trees against a large hill. Log cabins and a working sawmill harnessed the power of a fast-moving elevated stream that can still be seen at Dollywood today.

Back in the middle of the country, another group of entrepreneurs were enjoying their own success and looking for expansion. In 1950 Hugo Herschend, a vacuum cleaner salesman from Chicago, signed a lease for a natural cave in southern Missouri. He managed Marvel Cave as a tourist attraction until his death in 1955 when the lease passed to his wife Mary. Mrs. Herschend and her two sons, Jack and Peter, began to make aggressive plans in anticipation of family tourists visiting the Ozark Mountains. They built a small Ozark village near the cave and Silver Dollar City opened in 1960. Sixteen years later their thriving park gave the brothers a desire to recreate their concept in another part of the country.

In 1976, Jack and Peter Herschend bought Goldrush Junction from Art Modell. Seeing potential in the location as it mirrored the landscape and culture of their project in Missouri, they dropped the junction and renamed the park Goldrush for the 1976 season. However, this name was short-lived as the brothers explored the benefits of further connection between their two properties. In 1977, the park opened once again under a new name: Silver Dollar City Tennessee.

As they did in Missouri, the Herschend family added thrill rides and continued to expand the mountain heritage theme of both parks. Notably, at the Tennessee location in 1983, the brothers built a water-powered grist mill. This was the first full-functioning flour mill to be built in Tennessee in over one hundred years.

And then, after Rudolph and hurricanes, train robberies, and Confederate rebellions, Dolly Parton finally entered the picture. In 1986 the local girl who made good had enough of her own hard-earned resources to realize a dream: to bring something great to her beloved mountains that would create a lot of jobs. She made the Herschend family an offer they couldn't refuse and became their full partner in the venture. And, she leant her name. Years earlier, while filming Nine to Five, Ms. Parton looked up at the Hollywood sign and remarked that they should change the H to a D. Those around her laughed, but as usual, Dolly had the last laugh when paying guests entered Dollywood for the first time on May 3, 1986.

It's impossible to accurately measure Dolly's impact on the park. Certainly, the other Herschend park in Missouri has done well without her name. However, Silver Dollar City did not have near the competition that Dollywood faced in the 80s and 90s. Within a day's drive from Dollywood were several large theme parks: Opryland, Six Flags Over Georgia, Busch Gardens Williamsburg, Carowinds, King's Dominion, and Holiday World. It's hard to imagine the small heritage park in Pigeon Forge holding its own against these giants without the media power that Dolly Parton provided.

Ms. Parton has something that very few in the entertainment world possess: the ability to cross-promote products. Walt Disney was able to use his television show to advertise Disneyland while using Disneyland to promote the characters of his films. Dolly, due to her multifaceted career, was able to do much the same during the early days of Dollywood. At the time of buying into the park, she'd had a long string of successful recordings and several hit movies. She was also the most frequent guest on The Tonight Show with Johnny Carson and about to launch her own weekly show for the ABC television network. As one of the hardest working people in show business, wherever she went Dolly was sure to mention her Dollywood at the base of the Smoky Mountains. And people listened. Soon, her name was synonymous with the American dream of building something great. The guy who owned Amusement Park X could show up at a newspaper and the publisher may or may not care, but when Dolly Parton arrived with news of Dollywood, it was interesting and sold papers.

Since 1986 the park has grown several times its Rebel Railroad size and attracts many millions more. The arrival of Dolly also signaled the creation of distinct themed lands within the park. Each land represents a specific part of Dolly's experience growing up in the Tennessee hills. (The lands and their individual histories can be found in chapter 3.) Under the name Dollywood the park increased not only in size, but also in amenities, shows, and events.

The 1990's saw tremendous growth in the diversity and quality of food choices. In addition to the grist mill that still produced flour for the park's bakeries, each new land opened with restaurants and quick-service offerings. Several theaters were added, three of which have fly-space capable of producing lavish Broadway-style shows. This time in the park's history also introduced annual festivals and celebrations. The park expanded its operating calendar to include the middle of March through the first week of January.

The summer of 2001 was a big season for Dollywood as a second park opened adjacent to the original site. Dolly unveiled her new water park, Dolly's Splash Country, complete with wave pool, lazy river, and multiple water slides. In 2004 the water park's name was changed to Dollywood's Splash Country. Further themed areas involving water attractions have been added over the years. In 2013, the first water coaster in the region made its debut.

On July 27, 2015, Dollywood's DreamMore Resort welcomed its first overnight guests. This massive full-service resort proved that Dollywood is truly a multiday experience worthy of guests' precious vacation time. It's interesting to note that this resort is located on a new road called 'Dollywood Resorts Boulevard.' Yes, that's resortS with an S. I wouldn't be surprised to see the construction of 'Dollywood's Butterfly Inn' or 'Dollywood's Resort of Many Colors' in the near future.

The history of Dollywood is far from complete. With the opening of Lightning Rod, the world's fastest wooden roller coaster, and Drop Line, a 230-foot tower, the park once again expanded its footprint at the base of the mountains. 2018 brought Dollywood an expanded fall season, a multi-faceted performance venue, and the new Season of Showstoppers. Wildwood Grove, the largest expansion in the theme park's history, debuted in 2019. This new land added a coaster, several rides, a large restaurant, an indoor play area, and an interactive Dolly-made tree. The newest addition to the park, 2020's Flower and Food Festival, proves that Dollywood is committed to providing something new every year.

However, more exciting than all of this, is the park's dedication to changing with the current population while remaining true to its historical roots. Dollywood seems to have figured out that young people like thrill rides. But they also figured out that those young people grow up and want to bring their kids to experience toddler-play attractions. Then, those kids grow up and their parents are ready to get away for some shows and good food. As the cycle continues there is no doubt that Dollywood will change

2020 DOLLYWOOD AND BEYOND!

countless times. Hopefully, after many fantastic years of mountain memories, someone else will be around to add to this history.

RECENT AWARDS

2005	Best Wooden Coaster: Thunderhead	Golden Ticket Awards*
2006	Best Wooden Coaster: Thunderhead	Golden Ticket Awards
2007	Best New Attraction: Mystery Mine	Theme Park Insider
2007	Park of the Year	Golden Ticket Awards
2008	Best Christmas Event	Golden Ticket Awards
2009	Best Shows	Golden Ticket Awards
2009	Best Christmas Event	Golden Ticket Awards
2010	Applause Award**	IAAPA**
2010	Best Christmas Event	Golden Ticket Awards
2010	Best Shows	Golden Ticket Awards
2011	Best Christmas Event	Golden Ticket Awards
2011	Best Shows	Golden Ticket Awards
2012	Best New Ride: Wild Eagle	Golden Ticket Awards
2012	Friendliest Park	Golden Ticket Awards
2012	Best Shows	Golden Ticket Awards
2012	Best Food	Golden Ticket Awards
2012	Best Christmas Event	Golden Ticket Awards
2013	Best New Ride: RiverRush	Golden Ticket Awards
2013	Friendliest Park	Golden Ticket Awards
2013	Best Shows	Golden Ticket Awards
2013	Best Food	Golden Ticket Awards
2013	Best Christmas Event	Golden Ticket Awards

Year	Award	Organization
2014	Best Shows	Golden Ticket Awards***
2014	Best Food	Golden Ticket Awards
2014	Best Christmas Event	Golden Ticket Awards
2014	Friendliest Park	Golden Ticket Awards
2014	Best Overall Production	IAAPA Brass Ring Award
2015	Friendliest Park	Golden Ticket Awards
2015	Best Shows	Golden Ticket Awards
2015	Best Christmas Event	Golden Ticket Awards
2016	Best New Ride: Lightning Rod	Golden Ticket Awards
2016	Best Shows	Golden Ticket Awards
2016	Best Christmas Event	Golden Ticket Awards
2016	Friendliest Park	Golden Ticket Awards
2017	Friendliest Park	Golden Ticket Awards
2017	Best Food	Golden Ticket Awards
2017	Best Christmas Event	Golden Ticket Awards
2017	Best Shows	Golden Ticket Awards
2018	Friendliest Park	Golden Ticket Awards
2018	Best Christmas Event	Golden Ticket Awards
2018	Best Shows	Golden Ticket Awards
2019	Best Guest Experience****	Golden Ticket Awards
2019	Best Children's Area	Golden Ticket Awards
2019	Best Christmas Event	Golden Ticket Awards
2019	Best Theme Park in North America	Golden Ticket Awards

*   The Golden Ticket Awards are presented by *Amusement Today* magazine. Based upon surveys completed by established theme park enthusiasts, the awards are given each year to the best theme parks in the business.

**   Presented by the International Association of Amusement Parks and Attractions, the Applause Award is given to one park every other year; it is the highest achievement in the theme park industry.

***   In 2014, Dollywood placed in the top five for ten Golden Ticket categories. This is a record for any theme park in the history of the awards.

****   In 2019, the Golden Ticket Awards combined cleanest park and friendliest park into one category: guest experience.

Butterfly Wisdom

Throughout this guidebook, don't miss the special sections called "Butterfly Wisdom." These bits of wisdom are reserved for interesting facts about Dollywood or tips to make your visit better.

Why a butterfly? You should get used to these beautiful creatures because all Dollywood properties are full of butterfly images. Dolly Parton has used the butterfly as her personal symbol since she started in the entertainment business. She loves butterflies because they are colorful, diverse, and don't hurt anyone. To fully appreciate her butterfly-based philosophy, listen to her 1974 hit "Love is Like a Butterfly."

GREAT SMOKY MOUNTAIN FIRE OF 2016

Before we continue to learn about the wonders of the Smoky Mountain Vacation Region, it's fitting to pause and reflect on the most horrific event in the area's recent history: The Great Smoky Mountain Fire of 2016.

On Monday, November 28, 2016, a massive wildfire nearly destroyed everything that I've written about in this book. I honesty wish I was exaggerating—but I'm not. The fire was *that* bad. Most of the United States woke up on Tuesday to the scenes of devastation being broadcast on all the national morning news programs. Perhaps you were one of those who watched with a heavy heart—I know I was.

Originally the fire was attributed to an act of arson committed by two teenagers. However, after six months of research, it was determined that the blaze was caused by a bizarre weather occurrence and the teens were cleared of all charges. (I'm sure those are two young people who will be extra careful anytime they camp in the forest—as should we all.)

It's not uncommon for small brush fires to break out in the Great Smoky Mountains National Park. These fires are carefully monitored and controlled by park rangers. In fact, fire can be a good way for Mother Nature to do some cleaning up. (Dollywood even has a whole attraction based upon the work of fire-fighting rangers—see Chapter 3.)

Though brush fires are common, a freak storm front that stalled over the mountains was very much uncommon. At 11:53 a.m. the national park headquarters received notification that a brush fire of two acres was burning in the Chimney Tops region of the park. All the necessary precautions were taken. Then, a dry wind began to blow.

Wind speeds soon reached eighty miles-per-hour. The storm front came from the Great Plains and lacked the moisture that Tennessee usually receives from the Deep South. When the storm stalled, a two acre brush fire quickly grew to engulf over 11,000 acres. As the sun set, everyone's worst fear was realized: the fire had left the national park.

At 9:04 p.m. the civil defense system in the area was activated. Sirens blared throughout Gatlinburg and Pigeon Forge. A mandatory evacuation was quickly ordered—but the fire moved faster than any human anticipated. Glowing terror never seen outside of a Hollywood film came racing down the majestic hills. Pigeon Forge looked up the Parkway toward their neighbors in Gatlinburg and saw what was coming.

All spare hands in Pigeon Forge were tasked with getting the buildings as wet as possible. Dollywood, containing many of the region's historic structures, was soon filled with hoses on the ground and helicopters in the air. But the flames still continued to race over the hills. At 2 a.m., guests of Dollywood's DreamMore Resort were awakened and briefed on the situation—flames had spread to the mountains directly adjacent to Dollywood property. Resort personnel began to move guests to safe locations. As you can imagine, a lot was happening at the same time and many heroes were made.

Within an hour, the blaze reached a hill that contains Dollywood's rental cabins. Several of the cabins, and their surrounding structures, were lost. The night dragged on and the fire consumed many mountain homes that were decades old.

Finally, after an endless night, the dry wind suddenly stopped and the fire was officially under control before the sun came up. But when the sun did eventually rise, the region was faced with the stark reality of what had occurred. Fourteen people lost their lives in the fire—an incredibly high number considering how rare it is for anyone to die in a modern fire. 174 people were left with serious injures and permanent disfigurement.

It's estimated that just under one billion dollars of damage was caused to the area. Pigeon Forge proper, including Dollywood's theme park property, had largely been spared. But Gatlinburg and the the surrounding hills had been hit hard. Generally, very few people in this region live in a town—most choose to build homes and cabins in the mountains. Many of these homes were destroyed leaving thousands homeless.

While human life and property are, of course, the most important losses—consideration must also be given to the region's largest industry: tourism. The fire could not have occurred at a worse time. The Christmas season is the busiest in the Smoky Mountains—even busier than summer. When news of the fire broke, people all over the country began to cancel their reservations. In hindsight, this was probably the best for all involved because tourists would have just gotten in the way of recovery. Still, their dollars were greatly missed.

As it happens with disasters all over this planet, there are always people who are willing to open their hearts, homes, and wallets for the aid of those impacted. Starting as early as Tuesday morning, all the dinner shows and restaurants in the area opened and served food for free. Countless tales of people helping people occurred. The local business community stepped up to the plate, as did the Red Cross and other government programs.

Then, Dolly Parton entered the picture. (We'll learn a lot more about her in the the next chapter. Just in case you've never heard of her before, she's this kind of local singer that a few people seem to like.) Dolly gathered a few of her friends and produced an online telethon that raised more than nine million dollars in a few hours. After adding her own donation to the fund, Ms. Parton contributed a total of eleven million dollars for relief efforts. This is in addition to the resources that the Dollywood Company was also providing for families in the area.

For some people, life in the Smokies is back to normal. For others there is still a bit of cleaning up to do. And then, for some, life will never be the same as losses are mourned and grief continues. But let me be very clear: **The Smoky Mountains are open for business!** It's possible to have a wonderful vacation and never even know that there was a fire—that's how resilient the area is. I assure you that the fire will have no negative impact on your vacation. The region is even more appreciative of your willingness to spend your travel budget in the Smokies; their hospitality is extraordinary.

If you are interested in observing the rebirth of the forest, the best places to visit are the two overlooks off of the Gatlinburg by-pass into the national park. When driving on US-321 (Parkway) from Pigeon Forge, the Gatlinburg by-pass is clearly marked and exits to the right. When driving on US-441 out of the national park, the by-pass is also clearly marked. There are two overlooks that are easy to find on the by-pass, each with plenty of parking. From these places, you can gaze at the acres upon acres of charred trees. Then, look down and see all the new growth already sprouting from the forest floor.

The Great Smoky Mountain Fire of 2016 served its purpose. Now it's up to us to learn the lessons and begin our own rebirth.

CHAPTER 2

ESSENTIALS

GETTING THERE

The Dollywood parks are located in Pigeon Forge, Tennessee, in the foothills of the Great Smoky Mountains. Pigeon Forge is on the eastern side of the state; remember, Tennessee is quite long and it takes several hours to drive from west to east. The nearest midsize city, Knoxville, is thirty-six miles to the northwest and Nashville is 214 miles to the west. Dollywood is in the Eastern Time Zone and observes the same time as Washington, DC; Dollywood is not in the same time zone as Nashville.

DISTANCE TO DOLLYWOOD

- Knoxville—36 miles
- Nashville—214 miles
- Atlanta—248 miles
- Louisville—280 miles
- Cincinnati—285 miles
- Birmingham—291 miles
- Raleigh—341 miles
- Charleston, SC—353 miles
- Indianapolis—395 miles
- Washington DC—483 miles
- St. Louis—520 miles
- Chicago—580 miles
- New Orleans—633 miles
- Orlando—669 miles
- New York—701 miles
- Houston—957 miles
- Minneapolis—1,026 miles

DRIVING TO DOLLYWOOD

By far the most popular way to arrive in Pigeon Forge is to drive. Dollywood makes an excellent stop on the Great American Family Road Trip and the closer you get to East Tennessee, the more of these families you will encounter. Most people arrive via Interstate 40; traffic can be considerable exiting the freeway, especially on weekends, as vacationers arrive and depart the area. (See Map 1: Smoky Mountain Tourist Region, found in the back of this guide.)

From I-40, exit 407 will be your turn onto Tennessee 66. Follow 66 for 16 miles to Sevierville, Tennessee. There, US Highways 441 and 321 will join TN 66 and become the main strip through the tourist area of Pigeon Forge. It can be a bit confusing because there are several highways sharing this stretch of road, but in Pigeon Forge it is officially called Parkway. As long as you remember that Parkway is the main strip, you don't have to worry about all the numbers.

Eventually, Parkway leaves Pigeon Forge as US 441 heads to Gatlinburg and is the most popular route into the national park itself. (For specific directions to the Dollywood parking lots, see "Getting Around the Area." Also, Map 2: Arriving at Dollywood, found in the back of this guide will be helpful.)

BUS/TRAIN TO DOLLYWOOD

Organized bus tours to the area can be an economical and easy way to travel. These types of tours are plentiful from many parts of the country and usually occur in the shoulder seasons of spring and fall when senior citizens are more apt to travel. Check with your local tour operator to see if they have a scheduled tour to the Smoky Mountain area.

Unfortunately, other bus and rail service is not recommended. Amtrak does not provide service anywhere near the mountains. Greyhound Bus does stop in Knoxville and operates a shuttle to Pigeon Forge and Gatlinburg; however, you will find that once you get to the area it is nearly impossible to enjoy the attractions without your own transportation.

FLY TO DOLLYWOOD

The closest and most convenient airport to the area is Tyson McGhee Airport (TYS) in Knoxville. I've been in countless airports on six continents and I believe you will be hard pressed to find another small airport as relaxing and beautiful. Of course, huge international terminals in the world's biggest cities offer many more amenities and conveniences. But Tyson McGhee, in comparison to its size, will definitely surprise most first-time flyers to the area.

Modern, clean, and spacious, the terminal offers travelers several quick-service food options and a full-service restaurant. There is a gift shop next to large windows offering natural sunlight that you can enjoy from rows of strategically placed rocking chairs. A changing exhibit of local artists is available in the main portion of the concourse. However, the best feature is an enormous waterfall that extends from the security lines toward the check-in counters. Water flows freely over rocks and foliage indigenous to the mountains creating a soothing sound and scent.

All major car rental companies are located on-site; their rentals are accessed via an easy walk to the adjoining parking ramp with no shuttle to offsite cars required. Tyson McGhee serves a smaller market and security lines are never long when you are ready to journey back home. The airport is thirty-six miles from Dollywood via winding mountain roads that will take around an hour. However, I find that it is just as fast, and probably less troubling, to take the Alcoa Highway from the airport into Knoxville. There, take I-40 east to exit 407.

Airlines servicing Tyson McGhee (TYS) include: Allegiant, American Airlines, Delta, Frontier, United and US Airways. Direct service is available from New York LaGuardia, Newark, Washington Dulles, Washington National, Philadelphia, Charlotte, Atlanta, Orlando Sanford, Fort Lauderdale, St. Petersburg/Tampa Bay, Houston, Dallas/Fort Worth, Denver, Minneapolis, Chicago O'Hare, Chicago Midway, and Detroit.

GETTING AROUND THE AREA

There's no way around it—if you want to enjoy all the attractions of the Smoky Mountains you will need a car. The area is geographically large and diverse; public transportation is limited.

Unfortunately, as disappointing and confusing as it may be, the Dollywood entrance is no longer on Dollywood Lane! Several years ago, a new entrance for both parks was created off Veterans Boulevard. While the new entrance is better planned and eases morning congestion considerably, it does cause a bit of confusion as Dollywood Lane turns and passes alongside the park away from the entrance. (See Map 2: Arriving at Dollywood, found in the back of this guide.)

At the intersection of Parkway and Dollywood Lane, notice the yellow house located directly underneath a large Dollywood billboard. This is the Dollywood Information Center. Here, you can purchase Dollywood admission tickets and ask any question you might have. I find it much easier to purchase tickets online or at the park itself. However, if you're staying in Pigeon Forge and want to take care of some business before you arrive at either park, then the Dollywood Information Center may be useful.

The easiest way to get to the Dollywood parking lot is to turn east on Dollywood Lane from Parkway (US 441/US 321). Follow the signs as you are directed from Dollywood Lane onto Veterans Boulevard. You will drive on Veterans Boulevard for a couple of miles. Don't get concerned if you feel that you are leaving town and entering the foothills—it's supposed to feel that way! (See Map 2: Arriving at Dollywood, found in the back of this guide.) Turn right on McCarter Hollow Road, follow the butterflies that are painted on the road, and proceed into the parking lot.

All vehicles enter and exit both parks from McCarter Hollow Road. As you approach, you will notice the parking fee booths. Cars cost $15 and RVs $18 to park for a day at either Dollywood or Dollywood's Splash Country. You can also opt to use preferred parking for $25 and park closer to the entrance of either park, or avoid parking at all and use valet parking for $38. After the fee booths, signs will direct you to drive forward for Dollywood or to turn right to enter Dollywood's Splash Country. You can evade the parking fee entirely by purchasing a Dollywood Gold Pass (more information can be found under "tickets") or by taking the trolley to the parks.

As you drive along the parkway in Pigeon Forge, you will notice covered stops for the Pigeon Forge Mass Transit Trolley. More than likely, you will see the green trollies themselves around town. In fact, the Pigeon Forge trolley system is the second largest rural transit system in the United States. The trollies operate on six routes and will pick up passengers at any of their stops. There is also a large parking lot at the main trolley terminal next to Patriot Park in the center of Pigeon Forge. The cost to ride the trolley up and down the Parkway in Pigeon Forge is one dollar. The fare to the Dollywood and Dollywood's Splash Country stops, right in front of either parks' main entrance, is $2.50. Another route will take you all the way to the Gatlinburg Welcome Center where you can connect to Gatlinburg's own trolley service. The cost to take a trolley to Gatlinburg is one dollar. An all day pass is available for $3.00.

The trollies arrive every twenty minutes and do provide transportation to both Dollywood and Dollywood's Splash Country. However, during busy times when traffic is heavy, the trollies can take considerably longer to arrive. You will need to consider your budget, time, and effort when deciding whether to ride the trolley. Saving gas money is a benefit, as is saving the $15 Dollywood parking fee. Just remember that the trolley is not as convenient or quick as driving your own vehicle. The trolley can be a great way to get around if your party wishes to split up and you only have one car.

As already noted, traffic on Parkway through Sevierville and Pigeon Forge can be a nightmare. However, you can avoid some, if not all, of this traffic by utilizing a few of the newly constructed back roads that run parallel to Parkway. Notably, Teaster Lane and Veterans Boulevard can be huge time savers. Get a free map at your hotel or one of the welcome centers around town; use the map to locate your destination and choose a cross road to take you to one of these side roads. Also, Google Maps via Internet and app is quite good at calculating the quickest route as it takes traffic into consideration.

It's good to be aware that traffic gets considerably worse in Gatlinburg than it can be in Sevierville/Pigeon Forge. As US 441 becomes the very busy and narrow strip through Gatlinburg's tourist area, it is not uncommon to be at a dead-stop approaching Gatlinburg in the middle of the summer and weekends in December. If your destination is the national park, use the Gatlinburg bypass to skip the town and arrive at the Sugarlands entrance into the mountains. The bypass is clearly marked as you approach Gatlinburg from Pigeon Forge.

BEST TIME TO VISIT

Eventually, juggling the schedules of work, school, and activities will determine your best time to vacation in the Great Smoky Mountains. Fortunately, with the exception of January and February, anytime of the year offers benefits for a vacation in the Smokies.

Typically, Dollywood opens its season during the third week of March. The park closes a little earlier during this time, usually around 7 p.m. or 8 p.m., and is also normally closed on all Tuesdays. After Memorial Day, the park is open everyday until 9 p.m. or 10 p.m. During select Saturdays in June and July the park stays open until midnight. Dollywood scales back its opening days and times during late-August and through September. But in October, the theme park is open late every night for Dollywood's Great Pumpkin LumiNights.

The park is closed during the entire first week of November, as it takes that long for hundreds of workers to string up millions of Christmas lights. Because most people want to experience the Smoky Mountain Christmas at night, Dollywood tends to stay open later during November and December. The park usually remains open through the first Sunday of the New Year and then closes until it all starts again in March. (More information on special events and festivals is located in Chapter 5.) As always, it's a good idea to check dollywood.com for specific operating hours on the day or days you plan to visit.

If your visit includes a dip at Dollywood's Splash Country, your options are a bit more limited. Dollywood's Splash Country typically opens for weekends-only during the middle of May. Starting on Memorial Day, the water park opens daily, usually until 7 p.m. Dollywood's Splash Country switches back to weekends-only during the middle of August and the last operating day is normally Labor Day.

How long should you visit? This is a personal question that only you can answer. Consider you and your party's needs, along with vacation time. Complicate that with budget and you will make a decision that is best for you. There are plenty of things to do at Dollywood and Dollywood's Splash Country to keep you occupied for at least three days. Adding to that a day in the national park, a day or two relaxing by the pool, and a day at other non-Dolly attractions can easily fill an entire week.

As noted, I have a lot of experience with theme parks. If you can afford both the time and money, it is always best to spread out your theme park time over a couple of days. Two mornings by the pool with two afternoons at Dollywood is much better than one day by the pool and one day at Dollywood. Fortunately, Dollywood offers several ticket deals that make it easy to affordably vacation this way. (More information under "tickets".)

Smoky Mountain weather is as diverse as Dolly Parton herself. Early spring is pleasant with a cool breeze coming from the still snow-covered mountains. Summer approaches rapidly, even as early as mid-April and brings the usual higher temps and humidity. Vegetation on the mountains is extreme and creates an unusual rainforest climate for mainland United States. High humidity is the general rule for summer, but evenings are surprisingly pleasant and more arid—all that vegetation finally stops producing its famous steamy smoke when the sun sets. Fall is glorious with cooler temps and spectacular color. Winter in Gatlinburg and the higher elevations is more extreme than it is in Dollywood itself. Pigeon Forge does get some snow, but it typically doesn't stick around for long. During January and February the Sevierville/Pigeon Forge Parkway is quite desolate as most attractions are closed. However, with the addition of Dollywood's DreamMore Resort and its spa, cozy winter nights are becoming more popular. Gatlinburg, with more snow and mountain fun, remains a frequent destination even during these colder months.

Without putting too big a damper on your vacation dreams, a discussion of Smoky Mountain weather would not be complete without at least mentioning the possibility of rain—it is a rainforest after all! It can and does rain anytime of the year, and yes, it probably will rain during your vacation. Fortunately, I've noticed that rain in the Dollywood area is similar to Florida: intense and short-lived thunderstorms develop in the afternoon. On all my trips to the area, only one time did I experience a two-day soaker when the rain never seemed to stop.

Dollywood is one of the only theme parks in the world to offer a rain check. If it starts raining in the afternoon and the forecast calls for continued rain, the park will make announcements that rain checks are available. The same is true for Dollywood's Splash Country. The announcements will give the location (usually near the exit) where you can get a free pass for the next day. If it's raining and no announcement has been made, you can still stop by Guest Services at each park and inquire about getting a rain check. Depending upon the situation, and the discretion of the host behind the counter, you may get a pass for the next day.

Usually, I keep an eye on the sky and try to avoid the twenty-minute deluges that pass over the area. If you worry that a rainy day might ruin your vacation, let this theme park enthusiast try to change your attitude—rain can be your best friend! Rain always equals fewer crowds. Larger coasters will close if there is lightning in the area, but the rest of the park remains open for you to explore.

I don't like the plastic ponchos that have become ubiquitous at all theme parks on rainy days; I find them uncomfortable and too warm. Use a park map and stealthily dart from place to place. Also, I've found that one of my greatest joys in life is sitting inside a theme park restaurant with a cup of coffee as I watch real rain pour over the fantasy. As the water flows down the themed buildings, the line between real and fantasy gets quite blurry and I smile.

Butterfly Wisdom

Schools in the southern part of the United States typically begin their year earlier than schools in others parts of the country. In 2019, the first day of school for Pigeon Forge High School was August 14. If you are from another part of the country, you can avoid longer lines and crowds by visiting during this time of the late summer. Just be advised that Dollywood's Splash Country will only open on weekends once the local school districts are in session.

WHERE TO STAY

As with time of year to visit, lodging is a personal choice that will require thoughts about the type of experience you want combined with the budget you have for travel. There are many options for every kind of traveler in the mountain area. I will provide general information about accommodations, however it is not my intent to offer a review of specific properties. There are many travel review sites, but with all my travels I find that tripadvisor.com still offers the most comprehensive reviews. Read several reviews for the same hotel, disregard the best and worst review, and you will have a fairly good picture of the kind of accommodation offered.

DOLLYWOOD'S DREAMMORE RESORT

On May 14, 2009, Dolly Parton delivered the commencement address at the University of Tennessee in nearby Knoxville. After joking that the path to success includes wearing a push-up bra and five-inch heels, Dolly revealed her real keys to success: dream more, learn more, care more, and be more. The address was crafted into a best-selling book and inspired the name of Dolly's newest Dollywood adventure.

Dollywood's DreamMore Resort opened on July 27, 2015. The resort is spectacular with all the amenities you'd expect from a major resort and a full-service theme park hotel. If you speak Disney, I'd call this hotel a deluxe property, comparable to the Disneyland Hotel in California and Disney's Wilderness Lodge in Florida. But keep reading; the prices aren't nearly as steep as the mountains that overlook Dolly's resort.

The resort is located behind Dollywood's Splash Country. The main Dollywood theme parks entrance is not the entrance for the resort. The hotel is located on Dollywood Resorts Boulevard, which is two stoplights north of the Dollywood entrance on Veterans Boulevard. It's not as confusing as it sounds. (See map #2 in the back of the book for details.)

As soon as you pull up to the massive white building and its welcoming front porch, you'll see a water sculpture dedicated to Dolly's four keys to success. You'll also hear Dolly's signature trill coming from hidden speakers, and you'll cross a mountain stream to get to the entrance. Resort hosts are positioned under the entrance canopy to help you unload and to park your vehicle. (On the resort map, this entrance canopy is called the "Porte Cochere." I had no idea what that was, but perhaps some of you are more sophisticated than I am.) Ample self-parking is complimentary, and valet parking is available for $15 per night.

Allow me to get preachy for just one second: Always tip the people who help you organize and transport your bags. A couple of dollars is money well spent to help these young people who work hard in the Tennessee sun and humidity.

After you enter the hotel, grab some complimentary lemonade and gaze out the large windows overlooking the pools and Smoky Mountains in the distance. If you arrive during the middle of the afternoon, there is a good chance a live bluegrass trio will be performing in front of the grand staircase. The check-in counters are to your left, and a resort host will help to organize a line if you arrive during peak check-in periods.

As you'll see, no expense was spared during the creation of the structure. In addition, no expense was spared to ensure that the staff was well trained and ready for your arrival. Dollywood executives, nervous about their first venture into the world of accommodations, were wise enough to know what they didn't know. They hired an outside firm to facilitate many of the operations required of a successful full-service resort. Consequently, my experiences checking in and checking out have been friendly, correct, and informative.

There are a lot of options for accommodations in the Smokies; I'll cover those choices later in this chapter. Just remember that only you can do your homework and create a budget that best fits your needs. However, as you calculate the true cost of accommo-

dations, remember that staying at Dollywood's DreamMore Resort provides you with certain benefits, including:
- discounted tickets for Dollywood and Dollywood's Splash Country;
- complimentary transportation to each theme park (saving you the Dollywood parking fee);
- exclusive entrance into the theme parks for resort guests only;
- package delivery from theme park shops to your hotel room;
- live music in the lobby;
- access to resort activities, such as storytelling, Camp DW, evening s'mores, several pools, and a fitness center;
- lifeguards on duty at the fabulous outdoor and indoor pools;
- complimentary fire pits and many seating areas;
- complimentary Wi-Fi;
- Dolly-inspired atmosphere that is new, clean, and creative;
- early entry into both parks on Saturday mornings; and
- a complimentary TimeSaver Pass. (I'll cover this perk in the next chapter. A TimeSaver normally costs $39 per person, per day.)

ROOMS

Amenities and benefits are all very nice, but let's start with what you want to know first: How many beds do I get, and what will it cost me?

There are 360 rooms and suites to choose from in several configurations. Regardless of room design, they all contain a microwave, safe, and refrigerator concealed neatly within a cabinet. Coffee makers and hair dryers are also standard. In what I consider to be a nice change, there is a steamer instead of the usual iron and ironing board. If your room contains bunk beds, these beds come with unique sleeping-bag-type bedding that is cozy for kids and easy for housekeeping to strip and wash. Guest laundry is available on the second floor for a fee. Also, the entire resort is smoke-free; three outdoor smoking areas are noted on the resort map.

Of course, each room contains many depictions of Dollywood theming and reminders of Dolly's "dream more" philosophy. Think butterflies, music notes, and quotes from this famous artist, entrepreneur and philanthropist. It's not overdone, and you'll appreciate the creativity and attention to detail in these touches.

To give you a place to start, the following is a list of room types and rates. In order to provide a comprehensive guide, two rates follow each room type. The first rate is for a weekday in October; the second is a weekend in July. These are all nondiscounted rack rates.

- Two Queen Beds
  $249 (weekday in October)
  $329 (weekend in July)
- One King Bed
  $249 (weekday in October)
  $313 (weekend in July)
- One King Bed with Bunks
  $249 (weekday in October)
  $329 (weekend in July)
- One King Bed with Bunks Poolside (These are the only rooms on the entire property with an outdoor patio. The bunk beds are in a separate room with their own television.)
  $274 (weekday in October)
  $359 (weekend in July)
- Junior Suite (These suites have one king bed, one set of bunks beds, and a sleeper sofa. Six people can sleep comfortably in this suite; however, everything is in one room with one television and one bathroom.)
  $299 (weekday in October)
  $385 (weekend in July)
- Family Suite (One king bed in one room with a set of bunk beds in a separate room. The room with the bunks has its own television, but these rooms do not have a patio.)
  $269 (weekday in October)
  $345 (weekend in July)

- Two Bedroom Suite (A living room with a sleeper sofa is sandwiched between two bedrooms. The first bedroom contains a king bed; the second bedroom contains two queen beds. There are three bathrooms and three televisions.)
  $589 (weekday in October)
  $659 (weekend in July)
- Reunion King Suite (A living room with a sleeper sofa and a separate bedroom with a king bed. The suite has two bathrooms and two televisions.)
  $409 (weekday in October)
  $695 (weekend in July)
- Dolly's Penthouse Suite
  This lavish suite sleeps just two people, but it gives them plenty of space. The suite contains several rooms that have been furnished by Dolly herself, complete with special memorabilia from her career. You can book the Dolly Parton Suite online. Depending upon the night, the suite runs between $999 and $1,300. So if your nine-to-five job pays more than just rhinestones, you might be able to stay in this special suite.

Remember, these rates can change at any time, and probably will. The rates I listed are nondiscounted rack rates. The resort offers AAA and AARP discounts. However, the most significant discount is obtained by purchasing a season pass. Gold Pass holders receive a 10 percent discount off the rack rate. Super Pass holders receive a 20 percent discount. (You can find out more about these passes later in this chapter.)

Dollywood's DreamMore Resort makes it easy to check rates online at dollywood.com. Floor plans are provided for each room type when you enter the booking process. A deposit equal to your first night will be charged to your credit card when you reserve a room. If you cancel outside of seventy-two hours before arrival, your deposit will be refunded. If you cancel within seventy-two hours of your arrival, the deposit is nonrefundable.

SONG & HEARTH RESTAURANT

A table-service restaurant, Song & Hearth is located on the first floor of the resort. The dining room juts out from the hotel itself and offers beautiful views of the outdoor pools and landscaped lawn. There is outdoor seating in the summer and indoor seating next to an enormous fireplace in the winter. Right outside of the south side of the restaurant is a dinner bell that hosts ring when Song & Hearth opens for each meal service.

Each day, a breakfast buffet is offered 7:00 a.m.–11:00 a.m. The selection is extensive with an omelet station and everything else you can think of to create a full Southern breakfast. You can even toast your own Pop-Tart! Waiters are available to serve beverages. During the holiday season, a special guest visits the restaurant during breakfast. (He wears red and eats a lot of cookies.)

A family-style buffet supper is available 5:30 p.m.–9:30 p.m. Items on the buffet rotate each night and can include: beef, chicken, fish, pork, breads, vegetables, fruits, salads, and several sides. There is a large section for kids and an even larger area of desserts. I've taken one for the team and sacrificed untold pain to conduct this research, but I can attest that every item is fantastic at Song & Hearth—the whiskey baked beans and hot bubbling fruit cobbler are my favorites. There is also a donut wall—it's a wall full of pegs that hold fresh plain donuts; there are plenty of donut toppings located below the wall.

The signature item during supper is Dolly's Stone Soup. When Dolly was growing up, her mother would often ask the children to go outside and find a stone to make the evening meal. Her mother always chose the stone from the kid who needed the most support at that moment. Then she would scrub it off and make stone soup. (It was actually vegetable soup, and Mama was wise enough to make sure the stone was absent—if they couldn't afford a potato, they certainly couldn't afford a dentist.) Dolly writes in her autobiography how proud she'd feel when Mama would choose her stone.

Right outside the restaurant is a lounge that is open 5:00 p.m.–11:00 p.m. Food is available until 10:00 p.m. The lounge also offers a full selection of liquor and beer, along with many creations made with moonshine. This is the only place in Dolly's entire world where you will find alcohol. (You can read about the local liquor laws in chapter 6.)

Also, all the food and beverages available in the lounge can be delivered right to your relaxing place beside the pool.

DM PANTRY

If you're hungry but not ready for a full-service meal, visit the DM Pantry on the second floor. Right off the lobby, this cafe provides ample seating on either side of the grand staircase. Pretty much all the standards are available here: coffee, muffins, scones, sandwiches, soda pop, bottled water, salads, soups, breads, cookies, pie...you get the point. Everything is fresh and made on-site.

The most popular item at DM Pantry, by far, is baked-to-order pizza. I've never had the pizza myself, probably because I'm always stuffing my face at the buffet, but I'm told by my nephew that it's amazing. (However, to be honest, he'd eat a rubber tire if it had enough melted cheese on it.)

In addition to the cafe items, DM Pantry also sells candy bars, nuts, popcorn, and other snacks that you can grab and go. There is a self-service fountain soda machine—you can purchase a one-time paper cup or a plastic refillable DreamMore cup. (Note: This refillable cup can be refilled at the resort, Dollywood, or Dollywood's Splash Country for $.99. In addition, refillable mugs purchased at the theme parks can also be refilled at the resort for $.99.)

DOLLYWOOD TICKET DESK

As you face the staircase on the second floor, turn left to find the Dollywood ticket and sales desk. Here you can purchase the right combination of theme park tickets for your needs. (Ticket types and prices for non-DreamMore guests are discussed later in this chapter.)

The tickets available at the resort are discounted. In addition, the resort sells multiday passes that might not be available at either park. Consequently, these tickets are only available at this desk and must be charged to your room. If you choose Dollywood's DreamMore resort as your hotel, wait and buy your theme park tickets upon arrival at the hotel.

I apologize for not stating the exact discount. I inquired about tickets at the desk and was told that the prices and options change depending on the season and the two parks' operating hours. Tickets in the summer, when both parks are open extended hours, are more expensive than tickets in the fall. When I was at the desk during the first week of August 2019, the very end of high season, guests could purchase a two-day pass to Dollywood for $87.

Budgeting for travel is very important to me. Prior to each trip, I always craft an exact budget of expenses. I will definitely call the resort a few weeks before my arrival to discover the park ticket discounts available; I encourage you to do the same.

The ticket desk is also where you retrieve your complimentary Dollywood TimeSaver Pass. I'll explain the details of the pass in the next chapter. When you arrive at the resort you'll get your key cards from the front desk. Bring your key cards to the ticket desk each day to obtain the TimeSavers for your group. It's a bit annoying that you have to stop at the desk each day, but for now, that is the system that is in place. (See TimeSaver under the Showstreet section of Chapter 3.)

POKEBERRY LANE SHOP

Pokeberry Lane, located on the second floor next to DM Pantry, sells souvenir merchandise. Shirts, hats, gifts, frames, blankets, and the like fill the shelves. The merchandise is all specific to the

DreamMore Resort, and you will not find any of these items for sale in the theme parks. Consequently, Pokeberry Lane doesn't sell regular theme park merchandise. (There is a rocking chair frame branded with "DreamMore" that I'm especially fond of. I hope I get one for Christmas.)

A pokeberry, the inspiration for the shop's name, is a sort of wild grape that grows in the Smoky Mountains. When Dolly was a preteen, she used burnt matches for eyeliner and smashed pokeberries for lipstick. If you'd like to take this same frugal approach to cosmetics, go ahead and burn those last matches you have lying around. However, you may want to stop there. The FDA lists the pokeberry as significantly toxic to humans. In this case, what's good enough for the queen of country music might not be good enough for you.

CONFERENCE CENTER/MEETING ROOMS

A full conference center begins near the Dollywood ticket and sales desk on the second floor. There is a small boardroom and eight large meetings rooms that can be combined into even larger spaces. The meeting rooms are decorated in one of three themes: the skies, the falls, or the peaks. Full conference services, including catering for all meals, are available. The conference services offices are located directly across from the Dollywood ticket and sales desk.

THE MEADOW

In addition to the conference center, large functions can be accommodated on The Meadow, the resort's large flat lawn. Located on the northeast side of the complex, The Meadow offers fantastic views of the mountains with the convenience of the facilities inside the resort. This place makes for a fantastic wedding. Someone should have one and invite me.

BUTTERFLY GARDEN AND SERENITY GARDEN

Near the event lawn, on either side of a fire pit, lie two gardens: the Butterfly Garden and the Serenity Garden. Each garden features unique seating and good opportunities to appreciate the landscaping and the Smoky Mountains. They are somewhat away from the Swimming Hole and are therefore a quieter place to sit.

THE SWIMMING HOLE POOLS AND JUMPING SPRINGS SPLASH PAD

There are some nice hotel pools in the Smokies, but DreamMore's Swimming Hole is the only one I'd compare to a Disney resort. Sprawling and diverse, the outdoor pools at this resort are fabulous.

The main swimming hole is heated and curves gracefully around massive stonework and falling water. There are several areas of different depths for every level of swimmer. One end of the pool offers a zero-entry beach for those (young and old) who need assistance getting into the pool. This is the only hotel in the area that provides lifeguards for its outdoor pools. Remember, it is a lifeguard's job to watch for the safety of your children; it is not his job to babysit.

Wrapping around one long side of the swimming hole is a small river. The river is partitioned off from the main pool and has a current. All ages enjoy floating on the current. Also, walking against the stream is a good way to exercise after you've enjoyed a proper Smoky Mountain breakfast.

If you stay during weekends in the summer, a DJ sets up next to the pool and presents a kid-safe pool party. Other scheduled activities occur around the pool and are noted in the resort activities guide.

Behind the swimming hole, concealed by a rock structure, is the resort's large hot tub. With beautiful mountain views and plenty of space, it's a fantastic place to relax your muscles after all that walking at Dollywood.

Off to the side of the Swimming Hole, very-young children will enjoy the Jumping Springs Splash Pad. It's full of interactive water features that don't require immersion in a pool. There are flowers, mushrooms, and all sorts of things that spray out water.

Because the resort is still in its inagural season, there is no precedent for when the outdoor pool complex will open and close for the season. I inquired with management and was informed that the outdoor pools will open according to the weather. Since the water is heated, DreamMore has the ability to extend the season a bit. Management hopes to open the Swimming Hole during the first week of March and keep it operating through all of October.

Lastly, this expansive area is home to the resort's playground. With slides, swings, and climbing structures, it's the perfect place for kids to burn off some energy without getting wet.

STORYTELLING AMPHITHEATER

Dollywood's DreamMore Resort is the only hotel in the country to have a relationship with the National Storytelling Center. A small amphitheater, complete with seating and performance space, sits behind the Swimming Hole area. Check with the concierge or review the resort activities schedule to find out when storytellers will present their tales.

During the summer, the storytelling amphitheater is fortunate to host rangers from the Great Smoky Mountains National Park. The rangers lecture about topics from the history of Cades Cove to the geology of the park's many waterfalls. All lectures will be listed on the resort activities schedules available at the front desk.

THE GARDEN HOUSE INDOOR POOL

Although most guests will use this pool during the winter, sometimes I like to have a swim without the blazing sun in the summer. This glass-enclosed portion of the resort gives good views of the backyard and outdoor pools. The ceiling above the pool is vaulted and high, creating a nice place to float. There are plenty of chairs and loungers in this area.

Near the Garden House you will find DreamMore's complete fitness center. It's especially useful if you plan to eat more than once at Aunt Granny's Buffet over in Dollywood. Also in this area is a large arcade room.

CAMP DW

Even if you don't plan to use it, it's worth your time to take a peak inside Camp DW—it's that well themed. This large glass-enclosed facility provides a place for children to play while their parents are having fun elsewhere. Themed like a forest, complete with toadstool chairs and trees galore, Camp DW offers all the services you would expect from a resort childcare center. I hate to use the word "babysitting" because it is so much more than that.

Art supplies of every kind line the walls. It's located on Dolly's property, so, of course, there are lots of books. Kids will also enjoy the games, electronics, and physical activities that fill the room. If you are interested in using Camp DW, ask the concierge for a schedule of activities.

DREAMMORE SALON AND SPA

There's no way Dolly Parton was going to open a place to sleep without providing a place to get a manicure. The spa offers all the pampering and services you need to have an enjoyable vacation. All the services and prices are available online, but for your reference, a fifty-minute deep massage is currently $105 on the weekends, and an eighty-minute facial is $135.

The salon provides complete hair and makeup service. Dolly often says that it costs a lot of money to make her look so cheap.

Well, at the salon you can get as close to her look as your pocketbook will allow.

PUBLIC AREAS, PORCHES, AND THE BARN

If there is one thing that sets this resort apart from all other hotels in the area, it is the great number of public spaces with seating. Simply put, there are many, many places, both inside and out, to hang out with your family.

On the second floor, a large living room sits on one side of the grand staircase. A few of Dolly's musical instruments are displayed behind glass on the walls. There are lots of comfortable chairs and sofas; the colors are warm and cozy. Downstairs, you absolutely must use the public restroom at the bottom of the staircase. (Even if you don't have to go, just step inside). The restrooms are large with the most unique lighting fixtures I've ever seen in the loo. (I had my sister verify that the women get to enjoy the same lighting as the men.) Outside the restrooms, you can find another living room area in front of enormous windows that look out to the pools. There are coffee tables in the shape of Tennessee! (If any state is a good shape for a coffee table, it's Tennessee.)

Outside, enormous porches stretch across both the front and back of the building. I tried to count the number of rocking chairs, but I gave up. The front porch offers a view of the mountain stream that passes under the porte cochere. (See, I learned!) This is a nice place to sit and wait for family because it provides the soothing sound of running water. On the back side, the two tiers of porches have fantastic views of the outdoor pools and mountains.

Surrounding the vast outdoor pools are the normal lounge chairs and tables. But look beyond those and notice the old barn on the backside of the pool. The Barn is a covered place where you can sit around the fire at night. It's comfortable and tranquil. Check the resort schedule to discover when s'mores will be offered—the s'mores are complimentary!

The rest of the back lawn is full of benches, fire pits, lounge chairs, and tables. Check out the unique butterfly-shaped benches. Around all these public places, guests can enjoy the tremendous work of some very talented landscapers.

Quick tip: it's not a problem if you forget your watch while relaxing by the pool. On the frontside of the resort, Dolly sings 24/7. But on the backside, Dolly only sings at the top of each hour—the rest of the hour is dedicated to a mix of contemporary country songs. You'll be able to get a fairly accurate guess at the correct time if you listen for Dolly's trademark trill and crystal-clear intonation.

THEME PARK TROLLEY STOP

The DreamMore Trolley stops right outside the main door of the resort. Free service is provided to each theme park during regular operating hours. You will be delivered to a special entrance at each park. Make note of the entrance because that is also where you can get the trolley to take you back to the resort. A sign at each stop states the frequency of the trolley service. On my visits, the trolleys arrived every fifteen minutes.

CHRISTMAS AT DOLLYWOOD'S DREAMMORE RESORT

Just like its nearby namesake theme park, Dollywood's DreamMore Resort goes all out for the holidays. You'll know it's Christmas as soon as you open your car door and hear the joyful sounds of one of Dolly Parton's Christmas albums. (Except when they play "Hard Candy Christmas" in which case you'll want to grab the nearest anti-depressant.) The holiday music isn't just delegated to the outdoors. Most likely, you'll encounter some sort of live musical group performing well-known carols in the lobby.

Speaking of the lobby, when you enter it during this time of year you'll feel like you've stepped into one of the holiday movies on the Hallmark Channel. Everything is perfect, decorated, and tastefully accomplished. An enormous Christmas Tree fills the grand atrium from floor to ceiling—it's lit with thousands of sparkling lights. The lemonade that welcomes guests during the summer is replaced with hot chocolate and frosted holiday cookies tempt you from the DM Pantry. Song & Hearth offers a nightly holiday buffet with roast turkey and holiday cocktails are available in the lounge.

Santa Claus loves to stay at Dollywood's DreamMore Resort and you will probably see him during your visit. Check the resort activists guide to discover when and where he'll appear. Just to be clear, Dollywood's Santa is THE Santa—he might sing, tell a story, do a dance, or mingle with guests—but there will be no doubt in your mind that there is a sleigh with reindeer parked on Dolly's roof. Kris Kringle is a frequent guest for breakfast at the Song & Hearth restaurant. In addition to Santa Claus, the resort offers many craft and art activities during the holiday season. All these offerings are listed in the resort activities guide.

The outdoor pools may be closed for the season, but the beautiful grounds surrounding them are all decked out. Immediately next to the pools, you'll find serveral enormous steel forms in the shape of Christmas Trees. These trees are full of lights that dance to choreographed music several times each night. The times for this light show are listed in the resort activities guide. During most of the year, I don't have a preference as to which side of the resort my room faces—there are great views in all directions. However, during Christmas, I always spend the extra money to secure a room facing the backside of the building. I'm a bit of a Christmas junkie (you'll learn more about that later) and I love to leave the shades open and fall asleep to the sparking lights.

Dolly's touches are everywhere at Dollywood's DreamMore Resort, and you will find it is truly an immersive theme park resort. Look for her in the curtains, light fixtures, and carpeting. Before you leave the property, take a stroll through the Dolly Corridor on the first floor and see a collection of all of her album covers. (One album is missing: the soundtrack for *The Best Little—er—Chicken House in Texas*. To be fair, it probably didn't fit well in this family resort.)

Finally, as you drive away, look to your right immediately as you pass the main hotel structure. You will notice a pair of iron butterfly gates that protect a concrete slab. Why does concrete need protecting? Well, this is Dolly parking place when she is scheduled to be in the area. I can personally attest that she does not sleep in her lavish penthouse suite, instead choosing to park her tour bus behind these gates. During my first stay at the resort, I was taking pictures of a sign, and I saw her get out of a van and walk onto her bus. She waved to me! (She also probably wondered what kind of a fool was taking pictures of a sign in the parking lot.) Two members of the Sevier County Sheriff's Department stood guard outside the butterflies all night.

You might not see Dolly or her bus. And you probably won't be guarded by the Sheriff as you sleep in the resort. But, rest assured, you will be one of Dolly's guests and will be treated as such. Be inspired by her accomplishments and dream of your own. That's what this resort is all about.

OTHER ACCOMMODATIONS

This book is about Dollywood, which is why I used so much space to tell you about Dollywood's DreamMore Resort. However, you must not get the idea that staying in this resort is the only way to have a fantastic Smoky Mountain vacation. There are hundreds of hotels in the area with hundreds of pools and all sorts of amenities. Most of these hotels are much closer to the action on the Parkway than the theme park resort. Some hotels along the tourist strip from Sevierville to Gatlinburg will be less than one-quarter the price of Dollywood's DreamMore Resort. Selecting one of these places will mean you are that much closer to having enough money to vacation again!

For several years, Dollywood has offered packages via its website for guests wishing to stay in cabins or partner hotels. Dollywood's Smoky Mountain Cabins are located behind the park and off of Dollywood Lane. In fact, if you take the Dollywood Express steam locomotive ride up the mountain, you will get a great view of the cabins as they rise high above Dollywood. There are a large variety of cabins from one-bedroom versions for two people, up to multiple-room log mansions for large parties and reunions. Each cabin comes complete with kitchen, living room, and hot tub; many cabins have game and media rooms.

Dollywood's Smoky Mountain Cabins can be quite economical, especially if you have a large group. You can also save money by utilizing the kitchen to do your own cooking. I stayed with my extended family in a four-bedroom cabin and had an amazing time. The views are unparalleled in Pigeon Forge as you wake up with Mount LeConte right outside your window. The amenities included with a Dollywood package are also nice to have. First, cabin guests get unlimited free parking at both parks in special lots that are closer than general parking. Second, cabin guests can obtain a special ticket that gives them unlimited access to Dollywood for the price of a one-day admission ticket. It's easy to price a cabin package via dollywood.com. Do the math and discover if this option works to your advantage.

Also on dollywood.com future guests can price vacation packages with several other hotels in the area. These packages come with lodging and tickets; the price will vary according to which type of hotel you choose and how many days you want to enter the parks. Sometimes these packages come with additional amenities such as free parking; however, I've seen these amenities come and go. Be sure to carefully read the specific package you are booking before entering your payment information. As with all travel, make sure to review the cancellation and changes policy.

Of course, many times the most economical option is to book your own hotel and purchase tickets separately through the park.

Starting in Sevierville and continuing on Parkway through Pigeon Forge, you will find endless hotels to choose from. There are just as many options in nearby Gatlinburg. When it comes to lodging choices in the Smokies, there is really something for everyone.

Although they seem to get fewer every year, small independent road motels do still exist. These are the types of accommodations that have been around since Americans began to travel to the national park. Many times, these are the cheapest options, but may also offer fewer amenities. You can rest assured that most hotels and motels in the area have some sort of pool. Since these properties are all different and have their own policies, it is important to do your homework before booking. Check tripadvisor.com and read through all hotel policies.

All major chains are represented in the area in some fashion, usually offering their middle-quality level of accommodation. For example, you will not find a Hilton or Marriott, but there are plenty of Hampton Inns and Fairfield Inns. These hotels, and those like them, are known for cleanliness, free WI-FI, and complimentary breakfast. Also, the national chains tend to have more liberal cancellation policies.

On Parkway, there are no definite areas or distinctive neighborhoods that group certain types of hotels together. Unlike Disney World, it is not true that hotels closer to Dollywood will be more expensive. This gives you the freedom to think about your vacation priorities and choose a location that is right for you.

Butterfly Wisdom

Now, we enter into a great debate: is it better to stay in Sevierville/Pigeon Forge or Gatlinburg? This is perhaps the first big decision you will make after choosing a vacation to Dollywood. Everyone seems to have a preference. I've stayed in both locations several times and have definite opinions that change according to the chemistry of those I'm traveling with.

Sevierville/Pigeon Forge is much closer to Dollywood. The traffic is less congested and all hotels have sprawling parking lots. It is a bit quieter, but Parkway is several miles long and you will find yourself driving for food and entertainment.

Gatlinburg is farther from Dollywood. It is a much more compact area; parking and traffic can be real issues here. The restaurants and shops are close together and it provides more of a party atmosphere. It is very possible to walk the entire Gatlinburg strip and explore while your car remains parked.

If I'm traveling with other adults and plan to spend only one day at Dollywood, I definitely choose Gatlinburg. If it's just my husband and me—and we want to relax by a pool and spend each evening in the park, then Pigeon Forge is a better option. When traveling with small children, Pigeon Forge fit our schedule and was easier to navigate. Now that those children are teenagers, Gatlinburg offers more to do at night within walking distance.

TICKETS

Like most major theme parks, Dollywood offers a variety of ticket options for your visit. Also like other parks, the options can be a bit confusing. Sometimes too many options can be too many options. But, as with lodging, doing your homework and calculating the cost of different scenarios will ensure you get the most vacation for your dollar.

As you read this section, there is one important thing to remember: tickets to Dollywood and Dollywood's Splash Country are not interchangeable. You cannot enter Dollywood's Splash Country with a one-day pass to Dollywood and vice versa. If you want to enter both parks on the same day, you will need a special ticket that I will describe. Again, unlike the CedarFair parks and some of the Six Flags, there are separate entrance gates for Dollywood and Dollywood's Splash Country; separate tickets are required.

Please note, all prices in this guidebook are actual 2019 prices and printed for your reference. Be advised that prices can change each season; prices do not include state and local taxes that were 9.75 percent in 2019. (Tennessee has a 7 percent sales tax and the local area charges an additional 2.5 percent amusement tax.) Hold onto your hat because it may surprise you that some of the price options went down when I updated this book! People like to think that there is some sinister theme park man in a black cape attempting to squeeze every last dollar out of your family. In reality, the theme park industry keeps a close eye on the marketplace. They know that you can't spend money in the park if you don't even come through the front gate—they adjust the admission prices annually to maximize park attendance by anticipating an average family's disposable income.

Now, let's get started with the easiest option.

A one-day ticket to Dollywood is $74 ($61 ages 4–9; $69 over 62) and will give you entrance to Dollywood for one day. Easy, right? Trust me, it will get a bit more complicated as we continue.

A one-day ticket to Dollywood's Splash Country is $49.95 ($44.95 ages 4–9 and over 62).

A two-day ticket to Dollywood, and only Dollywood, is $94 ($81 ages 4–9; $89 over 62). The two days do not have to be used consecutively, but the second day must occur within five operating days after the first.

A two-day ticket to Dollywood's Splash Country is $79.95 ($74.95 ages 4–9 and over 62). The same five operating day rule applies to Dollywood's Splash Country.

As with most theme parks, the more you visit—the less each day will cost. This is especially nice for people that want to visit Dollywood for multiple short visits instead of one massive theme park day. A three-day ticket to Dollywood is $104 ($91 ages 4–9; $99 over 62). The three days must occur within five operating days, but do not have to be consecutive. A three-day ticket to Dollywood's Splash Country is $79.95 ($74.95 ages 4–9 and over 62).

So, now, it's August 4, 95 degrees with high humidity, and you want to spend the day in the scenic lazy river at Dollywood's Splash Country. But, the sun eventually sets and an incredibly pleasant evening begins...you decide to have dinner at Dollywood and stay for the nightly fireworks. You will need a pass that allows you to visit both parks on the same day.

A one-day ticket to both Dollywood and Dollywood's Splash Country is $84 ($71 ages 4–9; $79 over 62). Two days at both parks cost $104 ($91 ages 4–9; $99 over 62). Three adventurous days at both parks will set you back $114 ($101 ages 4–9; $109 over 62). As with all the multi-day tickets, all days must be used within five operating days, but do not have to be consecutive.

Most tourists to the area do not even consider purchasing a season pass when they are only going to be in the Smokies for a week or so. However, keep an open mind and do your homework. Sometimes, especially at Dollywood, discounts and other perks make season passes quite attractive.

A season pass to Dollywood is $134 ($124 ages 4–9; $114 over 62). Notice, I said Dollywood and not Dollywood's Splash Country. When you purchase the pass you must declare which park the pass is to be used at for the whole season. If you have a Dollywood season pass, it is good for as many days as you want from March through January—at Dollywood only. If you decide one day in July that you want to visit Dollywood's Splash Country, your season pass will not be sufficient and you will need to purchase another ticket. During summer, Dollywood opens one hour early each Saturday for Dollywood Season Pass holders. Only one ride is open during this special hour, but you can check dollywood.com for a schedule of which ride is open early on the Saturday you plan to visit. Dollywood offers a few incentives to those who purchase their season pass during the previous year's December. These include the ability to split the pass payment into monthly installments and a couple of one-day tickets to give to your friends.

A season pass to Dollywood's Splash Country, and Dollywood's Splash Country only, is $109 ($99 ages 4-11; no senior option). This pass is only good for those who only want to go to Dollywood's Splash Country on multiple days. (If you want multiple days at both parks, do not purchase two season passes. Keep reading as there are better options.)

To make things a bit more confusing, and to give you an opportunity to potentially save some money, Dollywood offers a Gold Season Pass for $209 (no child option; $189 over 62). A gold pass will give you unlimited access to Dollywood for the whole season, plus free parking and 20 percent off anything you purchase. Depending upon how many days you would park, and how much food, drinks, and merchandise you buy, the gold pass can be a very good deal—a 20 percent discount counts up in a hurry. Plus, gold pass holders receive 10 percent off rates at Dollywood's DreamMore Resort. Once again, only you can do the homework for your party. Remember, this pass is good for only one of the two parks.

A Gold Season Pass for Dollywood's Splash Country is $184 (no child and senior options). This pass allows you to visit Dollywood's Splash Country for their entire season, plus grants free parking and a 20 percent discount on all purchases at Dollywood's Splash Country only. It also grants holders a 10 percent discount at Dollywood's DreamMore Resort.

MICHAEL FRIDGEN

Hold on now...we're almost done. What about a season pass that allows visits to both parks? Well, that's called a Dollywood Two-Park Super Pass. This flexible pass gives access to both parks any day during the season for $184 ($174 ages 4–11; no senior option). A super pass does not come with free parking or any park discount; however, the super pass holder does get 20 percent off rates at Dollywood's DreamMore Resort. (Again, a 20 percent discount at the resort can save you a bunch of money and may make a Super Pass well worth your money.)

What? Now you want a pass that gives admission to both parks, free parking, 20 percent off all purchases at both parks AND a 20 percent discount on rates at Dollywood's DreamMore Resort? That's called a Dollywood Two-Park Super Gold Pass and will set you back $259 (all ages). You may be overwhelmed by these last options, but stay diligent and do the math. Believe it or not, there have been times when a Dollywood Two-Park Super Gold Pass has been our most economical option, especially if we play to stay at Dollywood's DreamMore Resort. A super pass discount at the resort, particularly if you require more than one room, can pay for the Super Gold Pass alone.

A special clarification about discounts at Dollywood's Dream-More Resort: it may seem counterintuitive because a gold pass normally has a higher discount, however, super passes reign supreme at the resort. A gold pass discount is 10 percent at the resort; a super pass discount is 20 percent. This is because the hotel favors those who use both theme parks. In other words, the money you spend at two theme parks is worth Dollywood giving you a higher discount than those that use only one theme park.

All the above tickets are easily purchased online or in person at either park. If you plan to obtain a gold pass and want to utilize free parking on your first visit, you will need to prepurchase the ticket online. Just bring a printed confirmation and show it to the parking attendant to enter the lot free of charge. You will bring the same confirmation to the season pass center located outside either park to have your photo taken for a permanent plastic pass.

Butterfly Wisdom

Not everyone in your party has to purchase the same pass. Once you're in the park, nobody cares how you got in there! Often, not everyone needs the gold option. Give one person in your party the gold pass and you will get free parking and 20 percent off purchases. Everyone else can use their nongold tickets and save money. Just be advised that only the person named on the gold pass can get the discounts; they must be in the car for the free parking. This requires a bit of paperwork and, depending upon the composition of your group, you may need to "settle-up" with the gold person at the end of the trip if they purchased things on your behalf. In addition, if you stay at Dollywood's DreamMore Resort, only the reservation holder has to have a super pass to obtain a 20 percent discount, but they can reserve multiple rooms.

When it comes to discounts and coupons, Dollywood is more like a Disney Park and less like your local amusement park: discounts are difficult to find. Dollywood offers a discount for active or retired military and special discount days for residents of Sevier County. Once in a while, local fast-food chains may print a Dollywood coupon on their cups. However, the savings will never be more than a few dollars and you can waste precious vacation time and gas money attempting to locate a coupon that may not even exist.

It's a good idea to 'like' the official Dollywood profile on Facebook and Instagram (it's the only profile that's simply named Dollywood). I have seen some special deals show-up on my newsfeeds. These deals usually occur when the park anticipates a time of low attendance. I've seen discounts such as 10 percent off or all adults pay the same price as a child.

Some area hotels offer discounted Dollywood tickets. After you've chosen your accommodation, check with the front desk and ask about these tickets. Again, the savings will never be more than a few dollars, but a few dollars multiplied by the number of people in your party may be worth your time. As you may have noticed, for me vacation time is more precious than gold and I will spend a few extra dollars to save myself hassle and stress.

Be careful of online ticket resellers. These types of resellers are a more common problem for the Disney Parks, but I have seen sites offering Dollywood tickets at a substantial discount. The problem occurs when you get to the Dollywood entrance gate and realize that your half-priced tickets are fake. A general rule of travel: if it seems too good to be true, it is.

There is only one official welcome center owned and operated by the Pigeon Forge Department of Tourism. The beautiful center is at 1950 Parkway and offers all the free maps and information you need to make your stay enjoyable. However, as you drive along the highway from I-40 through Sevierville and Pigeon Forge, you will notice several other welcome centers that advertise discounted tickets to area attractions. Be careful of purchasing tickets at any of these nonofficial welcome centers. Generally, they are selling legitimate tickets, but the savings may not be as substantial as they want you to believe...often, you are actually paying more. Make sure to compare the price of the exact ticket type they are offering with the published ticket price on dollywood.com. In other words, make sure to compare apples to apples. Don't pay for something you don't need or want simply because they bundled it together with other tickets. And, most importantly, always ask if there is a service fee. Most of these welcome centers have to make money some way and they do it by selling you a Dollywood ticket that is 25 percent cheaper. They've actually purchased the tickets for full-price and will now tack on a service fee that conveniently covers the difference in price, plus a few extra bucks for their pockets. Again, if it seems too good to be true, it probably is.

Although it seems to have gotten better in recent years, salespeople pushing timeshares are present throughout the entire area. Most likely, you will encounter them on the tourist strip in Gatlinburg, or while filling up your car in Pigeon Forge. The salespeople will approach you and ask if you are going to be around for a few days. Then, they will offer free tickets to area attractions in exchange for your participation in a timeshare sales pitch. The tickets will be real and are absolutely free—strict state laws govern this practice. However, you will be required to have a tour of their property and sit through a multi-hour sales presentation. Again, it's up to you to decide if it's worth your time and effort. If you decide to partake, be assertive and make sure they hold up their end of the bargain. Ask exactly how long you will need to stay before the free tickets are handed over. When the time comes, assertively remind them that you're ready to begin your vacation and request the tickets.

WHAT TO PACK

The Smoky Mountain tourist area embraces relaxation and fun. You will not need any sort of dressy attire. Even at the nicer restaurants, jeans or shorts and T-shirts are acceptable. Also, refrain from packing any type of clothing with offensive or controversial messages. Like Disney World and most other theme parks, Dollywood enforces a dress code in order to make everyone comfortable in the park. Obviously, swimsuits are fine at Dollywood's Splash Country, but they are not proper attire at Dollywood.

During the summer, pack lots of shorts and T-shirts. The humidity is intense and it's nice to have a clean shirt for each day. Because the area is a family destination, most hotels have guest laundry on the premise. As with any vacation that includes a theme park, comfortable walking shoes are a must. On a recent trip I wore a tracker to calculate the number of steps I walked on a typical Dollywood day. It recorded slightly over 30,000!

Also in summer, pack plenty of sunscreen and make sure to use it daily. Don't risk ruining your vacation by getting a nasty sunburn at Dollywood's Splash Country. In fact, while you're there, look around and you will see plenty of people who did not heed this warning. Be glad you're not them and reapply.

Bug spray is not required in the Sevierville/Pigeon Forge tourist area, including Dollywood. I've spent a lot of twilight time on the tourist strip and have never had a problem with bugs. However, if you journey into the mountains, you will definitely need some protection from bugs in the evening. If you've forgotten anything, there are the usual big-box stores and pharmacies located along Parkway; just ask at your hotel front desk for recommendations.

Since the spring and fall weather can be unpredictable, it's best to dress in layers. Shorts and T-shirt may be fine for an October day, but at night you may wish you had on a pair of jeans and light jacket.

If you want to enjoy the amazing Smoky Mountain Christmas, bring a heavier coat with you into the park. At night, it is not unusual for the temperature to dip into the 40s. The millions of lights must be viewed in the dark and nobody wants to shiver and suffer. Check the exact weather forecast the day before your departure and remember to pack gloves and hat, especially if any sort of December precipitation is predicted.

After clothing and other necessities like sunscreen and medication, let your budget determine what else you want to pack. If you have the room, you can save a lot of money by bringing your own food. Look for a hotel with a kitchen if that is important to you. However, even if you don't have access to a kitchen, there are many parks in the area with tables, grills, and restrooms. Patriot Park in central Pigeon Forge is especially large, clean, and scenic with the Little Pigeon River flowing through. Patriot Park is close enough to Dollywood to be useful as a midday picnic spot if you want to leave the park. Also, Great Smoky Mountains National Park contains many unbelievably beautiful picnic areas. These areas are easily accessible and noted on all official park maps. In addition to saving a lot of money, cooking your own food can be a lot of fun! My family has spent many vacation days traveling without entering a restaurant even once. Frying your own pancakes on a grill will cost just a fraction of the price they will be at a pancake house. In addition, kids can go crazy and run around as much as they want at a picnic site. It may seem like a lot of work, but the more you vacation this way, the easier it will become. You will be surprised at how effortlessly you can set-up, cook, and clean with fresh air and trees as your restaurant.

Bring some cash for smaller purchases and snacks, but you won't need too much. Credit and debit cards are accepted at all Dollywood locations and in most every other tourist location in the area. Cash can be lost and is not replaceable; credit cards are the safest and easiest form of currency for travel. Theme parks remain one of the safest places to visit in the United States. Criminal activity, including theft, is not a problem on Dollywood property and everyone must pass through a security check to enter either park. Still, be aware of yourself and your personal items at all times and don't flaunt cash.

And lastly, make sure to pack your swimsuit and beach towel. You will need both at Dollywood's Splash Country. Even if you don't plan on swimming, the towel will come in handy to save your lounge chair if you have to leave it.

Butterfly Wisdom

My sister hates to pack beach towels for her family because they are large and bulky. Seriously, five beach towels can fill an entire suitcase! Plus, she knows how easily kids can lose these things. So, when she arrives in town, she makes a quick stop at a local big box store. Beach towels, especially plain colors, are often priced well at these kinds of stores and can be purchased for as low as $4. When our week of fun is over, my sister folds the towels nicely and leaves them in the hotel room. She attaches a note asking housekeeping to launder the towels and donate them to a local charity. Now, we don't know what exactly happens to the towels, but even if the housekeeper or hotel keeps them, they are still being put to good use!

WHO THE HECK IS THIS DOLLY PARTON ANYWAY?

The last piece of essential information you need, and believe me, it is absolutely essential: Dolly Parton. Very few people in our culture would be able to pull-off their own theme park. Would you go to CelineWorld or MadonnaLand? CelineWorld seems like it would be too boring and MadonnaLand seems a little too...not boring. In order to make it work you have to be famous and wealthy enough to draw attention to yourself. However, you have to exist somewhere between good and bad. You must be bad enough that the place is fun, but good enough that people are willing to spend their hard-earned cash on your name. I can think of only two people who have been able to do it successfully long-term: Walt Disney and Dolly Parton. (While Walt's parks have been around for sixty years, he was alive for only eleven of them. Dolly has had to maintain her living Dollywood image for thirty years and counting.)

Dolly Rebecca Parton was born on January 19, 1946. She was the fourth of twelve children born to a sharecropper in the hills of East Tennessee. As she describes in several of her songs, times were tough for the very poor family that lived in a two-room house on Locust Ridge.

For someone who grew up to be such a huge supporter of education and literacy, Dolly did not have pleasant experiences at her own one-room schoolhouse. Quality and caring teachers were hard to find in the area and the environment was rough. Dolly captures this time so well in her timeless song "Coat of Many Colors."

But, Dolly had a huge asset that very few have. (No, I'm not talking about those...they didn't develop until later.) Dolly's brain was prewired for rhyme. She could quickly turn an ordinary phrase into poetry. Sometimes it was silly, sometimes it was annoying, and sometimes it was beautiful. Regardless, people were captivated and interested in her unique talent. Dolly Parton, the prolific songwriter, was born.

So, Dolly rhymed and enchanted enough to obtain a reoccurring guest spot on a local television program. She sang and played guitar on the show and continued life as a normal Smoky Mountain teenager. (You will have to read her autobiography, *Dolly: My Life and Other Unfinished Business*, to find out what a normal Smoky Mountain teenager was like.)

The day after graduating from Sevierville High School, Dolly packed some grocery bags full of clothes and got a ride with a relative to Nashville. Success was not instant, but eventually people took notice of the beautiful young woman with the clear voice and instant rhyme. Finally, her first big break occurred when she was hired as the female singer on "The Porter Wagoner Show." These types of variety shows were extremely popular in 1967. Porter and Dolly had a string of very successful duets that were promoted on the show.

In the early 1970s, Dolly began recording solo albums using material she wrote herself. Several of these recordings became enormously popular in the United States and caused some jealousy from partner Porter Wagoner. In 1974, Dolly said goodbye to Porter by writing her immortal ballade "I Will Always Love You."

The late 70s found Dolly's transition out of country music as she promoted herself in Los Angeles. In 1977 she had her first mainstream pop hit with "Here You Come Again." In the early 1980's Dolly's career and fame skyrocketed into the stratosphere. Her performance and music for the film *Nine to Five* got her on every magazine cover and earned an Oscar nomination. Dolly remained the queen of tabloid papers while she starred in several more hit movies including *The Best Little Whorehouse in Texas* and *Steel Magnolias*. "Islands in the Stream," her 1983 duet with Kenny Rogers, proved that she could be number one with both country and mainstream audiences.

Speaking of "I Will Always Love You," Dolly famously denied Elvis Presley the right to record her song. Elvis required ownership of all songs he sang and Dolly would simply not sell something so precious to her. Undoubtedly the King, who had never been told "no" by a woman before, was furious. (This story is told with photographs on a wall in Red's Dine-In at Jukebox Junction inside Dollywood.) But, again Dolly had the last laugh. In 1992 Whitney Houston recorded a version of the song for her movie *The Bodyguard*. The soundtrack went on to become the highest selling soundtrack of all time with 45 million copies sold worldwide. As if that wasn't enough, Houston's single of Dolly's song sold an additional 12 million copies. Dolly, who retained the rights and royalties, received a cut of each copy sold.

Dolly, the business entrepreneur, was born with the purchase of her share of Dollywood in 1986. Today, the Dollywood Company and Herschend Family Entertainment operate multiple theme parks, attractions, and dinner experiences in the United States. Dolly continues to own several recording labels. While religiously holding onto her own catalog of songs, Dolly strategically purchases the rights to other artists' work for the benefit of both parties. Her television and movie production company, Sandollar

2020 DOLLYWOOD AND BEYOND!

Productions, has a long history of creating stories for the big and small screens. Among its many productions was the highly successful television series, *Buffy, the Vampire Slayer.*

Musically, the late 90s to the present has found Dolly returning to her roots. Using her own labels, Dolly produced a series of critically acclaimed bluegrass albums. As popular as she remains in the United States, Dolly's music is even more popular abroad. She continues to tour in Western Europe and Australia. In July 2014, Dolly set the attendance record at the famous Glastonbury Music Festival in the United Kingdom by drawing over 170,000 fans during a single performance.

Never gone too long from Hollywood, her NBC 2015 television movie, *Dolly Parton's Coat of Many Colors*, was the highest rated network television movie of the past ten years. It's 2016 sequel, *Dolly Parton's Christmas of Many Colors: Circle of Love*, gained a similar audience and was nominated for a 2017 Emmy Award. Dolly is under contract to produce two more television movies and one variety show for NBC. In November of 2019 she debuted *Heartstrings*, a Netflix series based upon several of her songs. That same month the television special *Dolly Parton: 50 Years at the Grand Ole Opry*, received the highest ratings for any show on NBC during the entire year.

She has won every award imaginable. Twenty-five of her albums are gold, platinum, or multiplatinum. Her sales top 100 million records and she has had twenty-six songs reach number one on the Billboard country chart. Forty-six Grammy nominations, the most of any female artist of any genre, have earned her eight Grammy wins. Nominated for two Oscars, one Emmy, and a Tony, she has her star on the Hollywood Walk of Fame. She was inducted into the Country Music Hall of Fame in 1999 and received the National Medal of the Arts, the highest honor the United States bestows for artists, in 2005. In 2006 she won a Kennedy Center Honor for lifetime contributions to the arts in America.

As if this all wasn't enough, it's Dolly's philanthropy that has cemented her status as a legend. In 1996, Dolly formed the Dollywood Foundation to oversee her new Imagination Library. The program began by sending a book every month to all children aged birth to five in Sevier County. Today, the Imagination Library is in over 1,600 US communities and throughout the English-speaking world. A portion of your purchase of a Dollywood Admission Ticket is used to further the literacy work of this charity. Dolly has given millions directly back to the Smoky Mountain area through donations to hospitals, schools, and public works. Also through the Dollywood Foundation, Dolly secured 11 million to aid in the recovery of the 2016 Great Smoky Mountain Fire. These donations, along with the employment her various enterprises provide, infuse money into communities that would not normally have a very high tax base. 4,500 people in the area are employed by businesses directly connected to Dolly Parton. This does not count the thousands of people employed by restaurants, gas stations, grocery stores, hotels—all types of businesses that only exist because travelers are arriving to partake in Dolly's world.

Dolly has smartly protected her private life by giving ample information about her public life. She has been married to the same husband, Carl Dean, since 1966. He is a bit of a recluse and is never seen in public, proof that opposites don't only attract, they thrive! (Seriously, if I was married to someone who had their own theme park I'd be there everyday and insist on having my own parade.)

At age thirty-nine, (you can do your own math, that's the number I came up with) she shows no sign of slowing down or stopping her work. Dolly engages her audience via social media with the presence of someone much younger. She remains a sought-after guest on television, and print publications know that her image continues to draw readers. Dolly still graces the covers of the tabloids along with horrendous headlines of one sort or another.

But, of all the things people close to Dolly say about her, it's usually her authenticity that rises to the top. She is unapologetically the person she always wanted to be. A true original and embodiment of the American Dream, Dolly is simply Dolly—when someone can be their own adjective it makes for quite a ride. I'm glad she welcomes the rest of us to ride along with her.

Butterfly Wisdom

You will see many images of Dolly Parton at Dollywood, but you are not likely to get a look at the real thing. Unfortunately, the hardest working person in show business does not have a lot of time to wander around her own theme park. Plus, a Dolly sighting would most certainly cause crowd disruptions that would probably have a negative impact on your visit. However, if it is your dream to see Dolly at Dollywood, there are a few annual opportunities. Dolly is usually present when a new ride, theater, or attraction opens. Most likely, this will occur during the opening weekend of the park in mid-March. Also on this weekend, Dolly usually rides through Dollywood during an afternoon parade.

Each fall, Dollywood usually offers a press event to announce whatever attraction or addition is being built for the next season. Dolly is always present at these events and rides through Dollywood during afternoon parades. Unfortunately, these events are not normally publicized to the general public.

The easiest way to discern if Dolly is in town is to look for her bus parked on the north side of Dollywood's DreamMore Resort. When visiting the region, Dolly always parks her massive bus behind an iron gate near the resort—she uses a mini-van for transportation around the area. (She LOVES her bus. Seriously, if I owned my own luxury resort I would certainly not sleep on a bus!) If the bus is there, then Dolly is around. If it's not, then—despite any rumor you may hear—Dolly is not going to make an appearance at Dollywood.

CHAPTER 3

DOLLYWOOD

ARRIVAL AND PARKING

To start your tour of Dollywood, let's assume you found your way onto McCarter Hollow Road and drove over the painted butterflies indicating the traffic lanes. Now stay in your lane until you arrive at the parking booths. It's time to officially welcome you to Dolly's World! (See Map 3: Dollywood Parking Lots, found in the back of this guide.)

After taking care of the parking fee, if applicable, continue to follow the signs and watch for the directions of parking attendants. You will notice the turn to the right for Dollywood's Splash Country. We'll take that path tomorrow, for now, keep on the Dollywood track.

The Dollywood parking lot is unlike any theme park lot in the world and should probably be listed as an attraction in itself. The topography of the area does not allow for the large, flat, black square, which welcomes people at most parks in the nation. Instead, the Dollywood parking lot is long and thin as it curves around the base of a mountain. The lot contains eight divisions,

A through H, with labeled tram stops throughout. Don't worry if you find yourself winding around the asphalt a lot. This just means you are getting closer to the entrance gate. If you paid for preferred parking, or are driving a group van/bus, follow the directions to lots G and H. (See Map 3: Dollywood Parking Lots, found in the back of this guide.)

The parking lot is clearly labeled with signs to help you remember which section your car is located.

- A = Apple Jack (Mostly disability parking.)
- B = Butterfly (Mostly Dollywood's Smoky Mountain Cabins and RV parking.)
- C = Cotton Candy (I like to call this one 'Colorful Coat.')
- D/E = Dolly's Earrings
- F = Family Fun
- G = Good Times (This lot is only for preferred parking at a $25 fee.)
- H = Home (This lot is for group parking of vans and buses.)

Park your car and remember exactly where it is; take a photo with your phone. When you exit the park after all the fun and excitement, you will need to remember how your car relates to the tram stop you are parked nearest. Grab your sunglasses, sunscreen, and anything else you need and head for a well-marked tram stop. (Those who park in G or H will walk directly to the VIP entrance without a tram.) If you are lucky enough to have a spot in lots A–C you may be able to walk to the gate—depending upon your stamina. However, not even the most physically fit should walk from tram stop F. You can't see the Dollywood entrance from stop F and will be disappointed at how far it is when you round the corner near stop D/E and see the beckoning flags way in the distance. Remember, a day at a theme park is almost always a day of increased movement; don't waste all your energy just getting to the gate. As you wait for your tram, take a moment to appreciate the beautiful poles of hanging baskets that line the enormous parking lot.

Disability parking is located in parking lot A. I've seen these spots fill quickly, especially during the summer and Smoky Mountain Christmas. Arrive early to park closest to the entrance. It is also helpful to inform the attendant in the parking fee booth if you plan on using disability parking. They will have the most current information and advice on where to park.

Parking lot B is usually reserved for guests of Dollywood's Smoky Mountain Cabins. You will need a special card, given to you at check-in, to activate the gate leading to this lot. People who have a gold pass park for free, but there is no special lot reserved for them.

The parking lot trams are efficient and numerous, especially during popular arrival and departure times. Once on the tram, enjoy the short ride to the Dollywood entrance. Please note that pedestrians are not allowed on the tram road; a rustic fence separates this road from the parking lot proper. Also, when you leave the park, remember not to walk on the tram road as it is dangerous and against park policy.

When the tram arrives at the entrance plaza, the driver will point out the loading place to get a tram back to your car. This is the only place where a parking tram will let you load. If you decide to walk back to your car, and then change your mind, trams will not allow you to board at other stops and you will have to walk all the way back to this place to catch a tram. Also, when you leave the park, don't despair if you see a long line waiting for a tram—especially during peak park capacity days. The lines move very fast as the numerous trams grab passengers and whisk them to the correct lot.

If you want to avoid the parking and trams all together, and you don't want to use the trolley, Dollywood offers valet parking. Just inform the parking booth attendant that you'd like to valet. They will take your money, $38 or $26 if you have a gold pass, and direct you to the valet area right next to the park's side entrance (the entrance also used by the DreamMore Resort trolley). When you are ready to leave, inform the valet attendant and your car will be brought to you within fifteen minutes. Valet might be a good idea if you have a disability, or if you are pressed for time and the parking lot is already noticeably full.

DOGGYWOOD

As you exit the tram and walk toward the entrance, look for Doggywood near the ticket booths. A yellow house serves as a posh kennel for your dog as you enjoy the park. No need to worry about Fido alone in your hotel, just bring him/her to Doggywood for a day of doggy luxury—Dolly style! Accommodations at Doggywood range from $25 to $35, depending upon the type of accommodation and length of your dog's stay. There are even individual Smoky Mountain cottages for dogs that require extra privacy. Doggywood fills up quickly and you should definitely make a reservation by calling (865) 428-9826.

Dogs boarded at Doggywood must have proof of current rabies vaccination. You must also bring a supply of food, but unlimited water is included. Dogs can be dropped off starting thirty minutes before park opening time and must be claimed by fifteen minutes after closing time. Also, you must be able to prove that you are eighteen years of age or older in order to board a dog.

Doggywood is another example of Dolly's philanthropic ideals. During the off-season, the kennel is used to board dogs from around the country that have been abandoned by natural disaster. Several French-speaking dogs from New Orleans lived at Doggywood for a time after Hurricane Katrina until families could be located. Doggywood was host to lost dogs after the 2016 Great Smoky Mountain Fire. Even if you don't have a pooch to board, it's worth your time to look at the photos of Doggywood on dollywood.com—it's just so cute!

Butterfly Wisdom

Speaking of checking out photos online, Dollywood is one of the few theme parks in the world to participate in Google's Streetview program. During a day when Dollywood was closed, the Google team filmed most of the park's streets, just as they would for any regular city. It's easy to pretend like you are actually walking around a deserted Dollywood. Just go to maps.google.com and search for Dollywood. On most browsers, an icon of a small person is located next to the Google Maps controls. Drag that person onto the map and voila! You are in a virtual Dollywood!

GUEST SERVICES

Directly next to Doggywood are the park's ticket booths. Make a stop here if you have yet to purchase your admission. Also in this area, notice the Guest Services window next to the ticket booths. (See Map 4: Dollywood Lands, found in the back of this guide.)

Any question you have can be answered at Guest Services. Don't be afraid to stop and ask about any sort of information or accommodation that can make your visit more enjoyable. Remember, theme parks count on your loyalty and love return visits. Also, this is one industry that lives and dies by word of mouth advertising. So, ask away—it's their job at Guest Services to provide you with an answer.

If anyone in your party has a disability, you will want to make sure to stop at Guest Services and pick up a Dollywood Accessibility Guide. This guide is updated annually and will let you know all the information you need about the park's various rides and attractions. Also, ask Guest Services to point out the Dollywood Disability Center on a park map. The Center is located next to the Dollywood Emporium and is a must-visit place if you have a special need.

I visited Dollywood shortly after a surgery to repair a running injury and required a wheelchair. Wheelchairs and Electronic Convenience Vehicles (ECV) can be rented right inside the front entrance next to the Dollywood Emporium. Be advised that Dollywood is not flat. You will be fine with a wheelchair if you have someone in your party who can physically push the chair up and down inclines. But take it from my sister who bore the brunt of the work, an ECV may be worth the extra money if you want to truly enjoy the park.

After solving all your problems at Guest Services, if you already have your tickets there is no need to stop at the ticket booths. Otherwise, purchase your ticket from one of the windows. There are also electronic self-service ticket machines next to the windows—I've found these convenient and easy to use, especially if there is a long line. With your ticket in hand, proceed over a lovely mountain stream that also curiously passes underneath Dollywood's largest gift shop to your left.

Unfortunately, similar to all theme parks in the United States, you are required to pass through a security check as you cross over the mountain stream. At Dollywood this check normally involves an inspection of any bags you are carrying. While I have encountered metal detectors at many other theme parks, I've not seen them yet at Dollywood. However, I will state that the bag checks at Dollywood are more thorough then at most other parks—be prepared to have all compartments searched.

Now that the unpleasantness of security is behind you, proceed forward toward the entrance gate. Have your ticket or pass scanned at the turnstiles and congratulations—you made it! (Directly in front of you is a large gold sign announcing your arrival to Dollywood. If you do not see the sign, you are at the wrong theme park. If you see a big fairytale castle, you missed Dollywood by 695 miles.)

As you pass the sign and convince your group to have a photo taken, look around and notice that you are in the first of Dolly's lands: Showstreet! (See Map 4: Dollywood Lands, found in the back of this guide.)

2020 DOLLYWOOD AND BEYOND!

Butterfly Wisdom

At Disneyland, park employees are referred to as "cast members" because they are all part of presenting a show. Walt, afraid of the reputation of carnival workers in the 1950s, had the idea that employees are more apt to provide quality service if they have some ownership in the philosophy of the park. The philosophy at Dollywood is that visitors are all guests of a Southern home; its employees are called "hosts." Since Dollywood is the longest-running Golden Ticket winner of friendliest park, you can rest assured that the hosts will treat you like family.

KEY

SHOPPING

FOOD

RIDE

MUSEUM OR OTHER ATTRACTION

SHOW

CHRISTMAS THEMED FOR SMOKY MOUNTAIN CHRISTMAS

SHOWSTREET

Much like Main Street USA at Disneyland, there are no major rides in Showstreet. Rather, this themed area serves to acclimate you to your Smoky Mountain dream world as you enter, and to say goodbye when you're ready to leave. Showstreet is a Victorian street from a town by the base of the mountain. The hillbillies live somewhere else, as Showstreet is the home to shop owners and probably the kids that picked on Dolly when she wore her coat of many colors. In Dolly's world, this is where the rich folks lived. But don't fret about that now because all park employees, your hosts, are friendly and welcoming.

Now is the time to grab a park map and show schedule (printed together in one brochure). Directly between the Dollywood sign and the entrance there is a large cart that is always well stocked with this important document. The brochure you're looking for is called *This Week at Dollywood*. It's a combination of map and schedule that is good for the current week.

Also, if you are celebrating anything, pick up a button by the front gate and wear it proudly. The buttons are preprinted with birthday, anniversary, and the like. If it's your first visit to Dollywood, grab the "I'm Celebrating" button. When the park hosts ask you what you are celebrating, tell them it's your first visit to Dollywood and get special treatment for the day! The buttons are also available at the TimeSaver Reservation Center.

DOLLYWOOD EMPORIUM

Change can be hard to accept at your favorite theme park and I still refer to this shop by its former name, Butterfly Emporium. You'll hear people say both names, but they are all referring to the giant store located near the entrance and atop the mountain stream. The most important thing you need to know about the Emporium is that in order to exit the park, you must pass through this store. Again, whether you are taking the trolley, walking to your car or getting in the tram line, the only way to exit Dollywood is through the Dollywood Emporium. The only exception is for guests who parked in lots G-H, valet parking, and those staying at Dollywood's DreamMore Resort. The exit for these folks is to the right of the Dollywood Emporium.

The Emporium sells the largest selection of Dollywood merchandise on the planet. You will find practically anything you can think of with the famous butterfly logo. T-shirts, sweatshirts, and hats are available in hundreds of styles and sizes. Mugs, key chains, Christmas ornaments, and picture frames are sold along with postcards, sunglasses, and flip-flops. Also, the Dollywood Emporium has a large selection of Dolly Parton, non-Dollywood merchandise. Her image and signature grace T-shirts and other items in this section. Of course, there are many Dolly CDs to choose from if you want to take a piece of the park's spirit home with you.

Although many items sold elsewhere in the park are also available at the Dollywood Emporium, not everything can be found here. Specialty merchandise, like fresh ground flour and pancake mix from the grist mill, can only be purchased at the place where it's made. None of the handmade items from the amazing shops in Craftsman's Valley are sold as you exit the park. But, don't worry about hauling these things around Dollywood all day. On the side of the Dollywood Emporium, near the women's clothing, you will find the package pick-up counter. You can purchase anything throughout the park, including the workshops in Craftsman's Valley, and have your package brought to this location. When you make your purchase you will be given a card that will state when your package will be ready at the Emporium. As you exit the park, show your receipt and claim your merchandise. The service is free and the pick-up counter is open until park closing.

CENTRALIZED MEASURING AND RIDE ACCESSIBILITY CENTER

To the immediate right of the Dollywood Emporium is the Ride Accessibility Center that I mentioned earlier. This is where people with different abilities can discover all the information they need to stay safe on Dollywood rides.

Also in this location, you will find Dollywood's Centralized Measuring. If you have children or shorter adults in your party, you will want to make this place one of your early stops.

Centralized Measuring will perform an official measurement of the person in question. There is nothing worse than waiting in a long line, only to find out that you're not tall enough to ride. If you get an official measurement you will not have to worry. After measuring, you will be given a secured wristband. The color of the wristband corresponds to a key that is located on the back of any official Dollywood map. Use these colors to determine which rides you are tall enough to ride.

Butterfly Wisdom

Dolly used to have her own currency for use at the park: Dolly Dollars. These unique dollars were actual tender that could be used at Dollywood. The design changed every year and usually featured Dolly in the center surrounded by whatever new attraction was being promoted. Of course, the treasurer of Dollywood, none other than Dolly herself, signed the bills!

Unfortunately, Dolly Dollars were seen as more of a novelty than they were actual currency. Because their popularity declined, Dolly Dollars were discontinued in 2016. (Disney stopped producing their famous Disney Dollars that same year.) If you have a few bucks worth of Dolly Dollars laying around—and who doesn't?—you can still spend them at Dollywood; they will be worth one dollar. Or, you can sell them on eBay for a lot more. Most of these dollars can fetch $10-$15 online, but some are worth considerably more. A rare 1997 $2 Dolly Dollar sells for $69.95. A even rarer 2009 $1 Dollar Dolly, the one with Dolly as a park ranger, sells for $79.95. (That's almost a 1,250% return on the investment—if I'd only known I wouldn't have spent mine back in '09 on a mug that I've since thrown away.)

2020 DOLLYWOOD AND BEYOND!

SHOWSTREET PALACE THEATER

The Showstreet Palace Theater, located directly behind the large Dollywood sign, is one of the bigger theaters in the park. The theater has a large stage and is capable of hosting shows that require sets and lighting. If you've seen either of Dolly's recent Christmas movies, it was in front of this theater where she opened and closed those films.

The Kingdom Heirs, Dollywood's resident gospel quartet, sets up shop in the Showstreet Theater during spring, summer, and fall. The four men provide tight harmonies during renditions of traditional gospel hymns and more contemporary sounds. During Christmas, the quartet usually moves to the Pines Theater in Jukebox Junction.

The theater displays its full capabilities—and full capacity—during Smoky Mountain Christmas. At this time of year, the Showstreet is home to a live musical version of the classic film *It's a Wonderful Life*. This is a large production show with elaborate costumes, fantastic sets, and live orchestra. The story is condensed a bit here to fit a 60-minute show, but you will see George Bailey face the anguish of disappointment and the ultimate triumph of a life well-lived.

As you will soon learn, all the singers shine at Dollywood. There are a lot of seriously talented people employed by the park. During Christmas, you will hear more of a Broadway-style sound than you will during the other seasons. I'll admit—I'm not a huge fan of the film *It's a Wonderful Life*, but I sure am impressed with this musical version. The story moves faster than the film and the singing/dancing is thrilling.

Be advised: this show is quite popular and every performance will be filled to capacity. During weekends I've seen lines form for later shows before the current show even begins! If you don't have a TimeSaver (explained later in this chapter) you should plan to be in line at least an hour before showtime. During weekdays, and times of cold/snowy weather, you will have a better chance of seeing the show.

SOUTHERN GOSPEL MUSIC ASSOCIATION HALL OF FAME AND MUSEUM

Next to the Showstreet Palace you will find the Southern Gospel Music Association Hall of Fame and Museum. Even though it's located inside Dollywood, the museum is completely maintained by the Southern Gospel Music Association. There are a number of displays inside the air-conditioned space including an animatronic gospel quartet and an early touring bus. You can also see costumes, instruments and a variety of video clips.

The main feature of the museum is the actual hall of fame with its stately glass plaques. The number of inductees you recognize will depend upon your familiarity with southern gospel music. Several new musicians are inducted into the hall of fame each September. There is a small gift shop inside with a nice selection of recordings to purchase.

FLASHBULB PHOTOS

In front of the Dollywood Emporium is Flashbulb Photo where you can view and purchase photos taken by official park photographers. Mostly, these photographers take pictures of your group as you enter the park. There is also usually one willing to photograph your group in front of the large Dollywood sign. These photos can be expensive; so don't be afraid to decline if you'd rather just keep walking without stopping for a picture. However, if you want a nice photo of your entire party, it just may be worth it because the photographer has more authority to arrange your group in front of the sign without anyone else getting in the way.

SPOTLIGHT BAKERY AND SANDWICH SHOP

As you turn past the Showstreet Palace Theater and head down Showstreet itself, you will smell this bakery before you actually see it. Even if you're not hungry, or aren't interested in this type of food, it's still worth your time to step inside and see the famous Dollywood World's Largest Apple Pie. These gigantic pies, weighing twenty-five pounds, are made fresh daily. I won't even begin to describe their size because they are just one of those things you have to see to believe. You can purchase a slice of the pie (weighing a mere 3 pounds each,) or, believe it or not, you can purchase the entire thing!

If you've been to a Disney park and are a fan of the ubiquitous Mickey-shaped rice cereal bar, you'll be pleased to learn that Dolly has her own version. There are no mouse ears here—don't miss the butterfly-shaped rice cereal bars dipped in icing with sprinkles!

The bakery and sandwich shop also sells all sorts of homemade baked goods. Cookies, cupcakes, donuts, regular-size pie, and muffins are some of the fantastic desserts you will find. If you want less sugar and more sustenance, freshly made sandwiches of various sorts are also found in this shop. The Spotlight Bakery and Sandwich Shop is a good place to get your morning cup of coffee or hot chocolate during the Smoky Mountain Christmas. And, speaking of Christmas, they sell delicious Christmas cookies that are made right at the bakery.

During Spring's Festival of Nations, the Spotlight Bakery is the place to find the best German pastry outside of Germany and Austria. Black Forest cherry pie, apple strudel and German chocolate cake are as delicious as they look.

SWEET SHOPPE

Across from the bakery notice the sprawling Sweet Shoppe. Strategically placed to make it easy to bring something sweet back to your hotel at the end of the day, the Sweet Shoppe is really a collection of three different shops.

The ice cream parlor offers many flavors of hand-dipped ice cream. The unmistakable scent of freshly made waffle bowls fills the air of the shop and the street outside. You can get your ice cream in cups, cones, or the fresh waffle bowls. Homemade shakes and sundaes are also on the menu.

The center section of the Sweet Shoppe is home to a large candy counter of freshly made treats. Everything you see behind the glass is made at Dollywood, sometimes just minutes before you are viewing it. The biggest seller has to be the homemade fudge available in many flavors. Cake pops, covered apples, nut clusters, and all sorts of fresh chocolates are begging for you to try.

The last section of the Shoppe sells prepackaged candy. You will find your favorite brands of candies and chocolate. However, you will also find candy sealed in plastic bags with the Dollywood logo. These collections of taffies, brittles, licorice, and lollypops make excellent gifts because they carry the unique Dollywood butterfly mark. Lastly, the Sweet Shoppe carries a selection of sugar-free candy both behind the counter and prepackaged.

One of my favorite areas, and a little known gem, is the porch that wraps around the front of the Sweet Shoppe. There are always vacant rocking chairs that make an awesome place to watch people pass by on Showstreet. I'm not sure why this shaded retreat is not used more; perhaps people are too distracted by the goods inside the shop to notice the porch.

Next to the Sweet Shoppe is the first smoking area you will encounter while in the park. Dollywood enforces a strict smoking policy and you must be in one of these official areas to smoke. Each land at Dollywood has a smoking area and they are marked with a blue 'S' on all park maps. There are also designated vaping areas noted on the map with a 'V'. Sometimes the smoking and vaping areas are the same, other times they are not—I don't know

Butterfly Wisdom

As you walk around the park, look for signs asking you to text for a coupon. These signs are usually stuck into small planters in front of various shops. The signs will ask you to text a word (often, something like "Dolly" or "Butterfly") to a number. Within a minute or two, you will get a coupon sent back via text. Sometimes these coupons are usable, sometimes not, but you won't know until you try. I've received anything from 25 percent off items at the Sweet Shoppe or buy-one-get-one deals at the buffets. Your normal texting rates will apply. Also, I've never received a text from Dollywood after leaving the park, so don't worry that you're signing up for a lifetime of butterfly messages.

THE SOUTHERN PANTRY

If you're a fan of southern cooking, then you must visit this shop on Showstreet. The Southern Pantry sells all sorts of food products for use in your kitchen back home. Preserves, pickles, butters, sauces, and spreads can be found alongside salsas, flours, and mixes. Some of the products are produced right at Dollywood and others are brought in from outside the park.

The best part of The Southern Pantry is the free samples. There is always a cart in the back of the shop where a Dollywood host provides samples of the various products. They offer the samples on small crackers. Anything in this shop would make a great gift (especially for me).

Most of the items here are not available at the Dollywood Emporium. Use package pick-up, or wait until you are ready to leave to make your purchase. The Southern Pantry is quite close to the park's exit.

SHOWSTREET SNACKS AND DINNER SHOW TICKETS

Across the street from the candy shop are two small structures. The first is Showstreet Snacks. This quick-service eatery offers snacks that change with the season. You never know what you will find, but it's sure to be delicious.

When you see large fiberglass horses, you'll know that you've found the reservation center for Dolly Parton's Dinner Show Attractions. It may surprise you to learn that Dollywood, as big as it is, is not the only Dolly Parton-owned set of attractions in the Smokies. Over on the Parkway Dolly operates Dolly Parton's Stampede and Pirates' Voyage Dinner Show. Both of these shows are owned by Dolly's Dollywood Company and tickets for them can be purchased here. (I'll describe both of these dinner attractions later in the book.)

Dolly also owns several more dinner theaters in the area including The Comedy Barn, Smoky Mountain Opry, and the Hatfield and McCoy Dinner Show. However, because these attractions aren't directly owned by the Dollywood Company, tickets for these shows are not available inside the park.

FRONT PORCH CAFE

The Front Porch Cafe is the full-service sit-down establishment on Showstreet. It's where the merchants' families take each other on special occasions, and now you can dine here too. The menu features home-cooked Southern dishes. This is the only restaurant in the park that serves fried green tomatoes and succotash. The dessert is a staple of Southern sweetness: banana pudding.

Completely renovated in 2016, when it changed from the Backstage Restaurant, the décor is contemporary Southern. It looks like your Grandma's house—if your Grandma is Julia Sugarbaker from *Designing Women*. It's a fun environment with windows to look at the action on Showstreet. This is the place to go if you are interested in the current restaurant movement to serve local foods. Much, if not all, of the food is produced within fifty miles of Dollywood. If you ask, the servers are good at describing where certain vegetables or meats are obtained.

During Smoky Mountain Christmas, the Front Porch Cafe offers dining with a special guest. None other than Santa Claus makes his way around the tables and eagerly poses for photos with guests of all ages. I know that Mr. Claus has many helpers during his busy December season, but I'm convinced that the Santa at the Front Porch Cafe is the real guy all the way from the North Pole—he is that convincing!

TIMESAVER RESERVATION CENTER

Next to the Front Porch Cafe, you will find the TimeSaver line management system. Many theme parks have some sort of line skipping pass available that allows guests access to special and much shorter lines. These passes come at a premium charge that can be as much as $120—on top of park admission! At Dollywood, the TimeSaver system operates a little differently and is considerably cheaper than comparable parks. (Disney is an exception to the rule with its various Fastpass systems that are still free.)

TimeSaver costs $39 and lets you skip the line for a limited number of attractions. After paying at the TimeSaver center, you will be given a sturdy laminated card and a lanyard—you can wear the card around your neck or keep it in a bag—just don't lose it because it cannot be replaced. TimeSaver allows you to skip ten

lines in the park on the day you purchase the pass. Each guest who wants to skip a line must have their own pass. When you want to ride, just enter through the special TimeSaver entrance and a Dollywood host will mark your TimeSaver card. TimeSaver works for these attractions:
- Barnstormer
- Dizzy Disk
- FireChaser Express (see next paragraph)
- Dragonflier (see next paragraph)
- Mystery Mine
- Sky Rider
- Smoky Mountain River Rampage
- Tennessee Tornado
- Thunderhead
- Waltzing Swinger
- Wild Eagle
- Drop Line
- Lightning Rod (see next paragraph)

With a TimeSaver card you can skip ten lines. You can mix and match the attractions as much as you want. If it's a hot day and you want to ride River Rampage ten times—go for it—but then your TimeSaver will be complete. There are three exceptions: Dragonflier, FireChaser Express, and Lightning Rod can only be ridden once with a TimeSaver.

If you want to skip more than ten lines, you can purchase TimeSaver Unlimited for $49. Guests at Dollywood's DreamMore Resort get the standard (not unlimited) version for free during their stay. Resort guests obtain their lanyards at the DreamMore ticket desk and not at the TimeSaver center.

TimeSaver also holds a front seat for you at Dollywood shows. The process is a bit different, as the TimeSaver card does not list shows. To reserve a show you will need to visit one of the show kiosks that are located inside the TimeSaver Reservation Center. Just select the show you want to see and have fun in the park. Right before the show starts, you can enter the theater through a TimeSaver door, have your lanyard card scanned and be seated in a reserved section. However, you must be seated at least five minutes before show time or your seat will be given away. TimeSaver only reserves one seat for each card. Each person in your party will have to purchase their own TimeSaver in order to use the system.

As with all these line-skipping passes, there is always one big question: is it worth it? Well, that depends upon your situation. I have never had a problem getting a good seat at a Dollywood show during the spring, summer, or fall. With the exceptions of Lightning Rod and FireChaser Express, I've also not had a problem getting on a ride without too much of a line. However, you should know that I'm an experienced theme park visitor and know how to ride early, late, and during meal times. Also, I've ridden everything before and if the line is too long it doesn't break my heart to skip it. So, for me, TimeSaver is not really worth it during most of the year. However, it is definitely worth it for my roller coaster obsessed nephew. He wants to ride coasters as much as he can—all day long. Even though he can only use TimeSaver once for Lightning Rod, he doesn't mind waiting in its long line because he knows he can ride Wild Eagle up to nine times without waiting in any line whatsoever. One of us usually has a gold pass and can get a discount on the TimeSaver. For my nephew, the TimeSaver is money well spent.

For me, TimeSaver becomes necessary during Smoky Mountain Christmas. Dollywood's shows are extraordinary during this time of year and their lines reflect that. Guests can expect to wait two hours to see shows at Showstreet Palace and DP's Celebrity Theater. $34 (the cost of TimeSaver with a gold discount) is worth it for me to have fun in the park and still get a seat in the front of the auditorium.

DP'S CELEBRITY THEATER 🎄 🎵

If you have to ask what the DP stands for, then you should probably start reading this book all over again. DP's Celebrity Theater is the largest and most technologically advanced theater in the park. Capable of producing full Broadway-style extravaganzas, the theater has played host to many country music stars over the years, including Dolly Parton herself.

For several years the summer season brought Dolly's own musical, *Sha-Kon-O-Hey*, to Dollywood. Sha-Kon-O-Hey is the Native American word for the Smoky Mountains. For the last couple of years, however, the park has not produced a fully-staged summer production in DP's Celebrity Theater—this is too bad.

Instead, during recent summers a show called *Summer Feels...* makes its home inside the theater. This show involves around ten singers performing country hits of the past and present. There is, of course, a live band because pre-taped music is quite taboo at Dollywood. (Are you listening Mickey Mouse? Many people still like live music.) It's a good show and worth your time to see it, especially on a hot day.

Every spring Dollywood celebrates its Festival of Nations. I've seen some amazing performances inside DP's Celebrity Theater during this time of the year. The Ukrainian National Dance Company is one performance I will never forget with high-kicking men and beautiful women gliding effortlessly as though they floated on air.

But, to see the complete technical capabilities of this theater, you must visit during Smoky Mountain Christmas. DP's Celebrity Theater is normally home to one of the more popular Christmas shows at Dollywood: *Christmas in the Smokies*. A talented cast presents familiar carols and mountain holiday melodies. The sets and costumes for this show are extraordinary. There is a bit of a story about people arriving home for Christmas—you'll see their town, train, and mountain cabin. There is a sleigh ride complete with perfectly falling snow.

As with all shows at Dollywood, the music you hear is live, from singers to the orchestra. It takes quite a talented individual to sing both country standards and holiday classical hymns. Dollywood conducts nationwide auditions every spring and they are always able to find the perfect musicians for this special show. *Christmas in the Smokies* is the closest you will ever get to stepping inside a Christmas card.

Special note: *Christmas in the Smokies* is very popular. If this is your only visit to Dollywood, and you have a list of things to do, I highly suggest purchasing a TimeSaver pass. With a TimeSaver, you will be able to reserve a seat at the TimeSaver Reservation Center. Then, you can enjoy the park and enter the theater up until ten minutes before showtime. If you do not have a TimeSaver pass you must be prepared to get in line at least 90-minutes before showtime. Believe it or not, I have seen guests line up for the 4:30 show before the 2:30 performance had even started!

Park hosts are on hand to count the crowd and organize the lines—please be nice to them. They aren't able to build more seats and if you can't see this show there are plenty of other wonderful Christmas offerings to experience in the park. On especially busy days during the holidays, park hosts will hand out vouchers that you can use to claim a seat for a specific performance without having to wait in line. These vouchers do not guarantee a good seat, but they will allow you to have fun in the park instead of waiting for two hours. Every seat is good in the theater—my advice is to take the voucher and explore the park until showtime.

SOUTHERN LIFE AND GAZEBO GIFTS

Outside the TimeSaver Reservation Center and Front Porch Cafe, there is a large plaza area that usually contains an elaborate decoration that serves as a centerpiece for whatever season Dollywood is currently celebrating. It's a great place to have another photo taken. Two shops also surround this plaza.

Southern Life stocks patriotic merchandise that is mainly centered around the geographic southern part of the United States. From t-shirts to home decor, southern hospitality is the rule in this shop.

Southern Life also sells items that portray positive affirmations. Again, the merchandise runs the gamut from attire to kitchen utensils—all with messages helping you to start your day back home.

Depending upon which time of year you visit, Gazebo Gifts offers items tied to whatever festival Dollywood is currently hosting. This is the place to buy your Great American Summer apparel and merchandise dedicated to the countries represented in the Festival of Nations. (For more information about the specific festivals, see Chapter 5.) Notably, during Smoky Mountain Christmas, Gazebo Gifts sells special Dollywood Christmas merchandise featuring the Dollywood logo with various seasonal characters.

Back in the plaza you will smell the wonderful aroma coming from Market Square. You may even see some guests enjoying meals on one of the many outdoor tables. Try to resist the temptation of Market Square, at least for now. Our tour of Dollywood continues in another direction, but I promise that there is A LOT of food to come!

Butterfly Wisdom

The plaza outside DP's Celebrity Theater is a great place to grab a photograph, but it's not the only worthy spot in the park. I've listed my favorite places to get that perfect picture here:

- Showstreet Palace Theater: Right in front of the gold Dollywood sign is the perfect group photo spot; there are always Dollywood photographers here to get the shot.

2020 DOLLYWOOD AND BEYOND!

- Grist Mill: In my opinion, the most iconic photo of Dollywood is on the side of the Dollywood Grist Mill. Stand in front of the pond and capture the turning mill wheel in the background.

- Dollywood Express Locomotive: Okay, I may have just lied. The most iconic photo of Dollywood is in front of the Dollywood Locomotive as steam bellows from its top. It takes a good thirty minutes to unload and load the train. You'll have plenty of time to get your shot during this process.

- Owls of Wilderness Pass: You can't pass these owls without stopping for a photograph. It simply can't be done. Tucked back in Wilderness Pass, two adorable owls have just hatched next to a large Dollywood sign.

- The fountain inside The Plaza at Wilderness Pass: Pose next to a recreation of a mountain streams as it blasts water high in the air.

- Log Heart of Timber Canyon: For the Romantics among us, there is a large heart made of logs on the winding path that connects Timber Canyon to Showstreet. The heart contains a Dollywood sign and there is often a Dollywood photographer here to help with the shot.

- Other Weird Stuff of Timber Canyon: For the Un-Romantics among us, there are several other objects, besides the heart, on the path between Timber Canyon and Showstreet. There is a coffin, graveyard, and a pair of Hillbilly showers. If your pre-teen has a phone and is exploring Dollywood on their own—all of their pictures will be taken on this path.

- Adventures in Imagination: You can't go all the way to Dollywood and not get at least one picture with Dolly Parton in it. Head over to Adventures in Imagination for these spots. Dolly's large image is mounted above the Dreamsong Theater and is your best bet for a group shot. You'll also find some colorful images of Ms. Parton along the side of Dolly's Closet. In addition to Dolly's bus, there are lots of Dolly-centric photographs to be taken inside the Chasing Rainbows Museum.

- Wildwood Grove: the spectacular tree in the center of Wildwood Grove is begging for a photo. The photographer may have to stand back a bit to get the entire tree. My advice is to go early in the day when the area isn't crowded.
- Smoky Mountain Christmas: Several holiday photo spots pop-up during this time of year. Jukebox Junction, with its fantastic retro decorations, offers large illuminated blow-molds that will take you back to a time when inflatable decor wasn't around. There is often a romantic mistletoe photo spot in Craftsman's Valley next to Old Flames Candle Shop. The floating Christmas trees on the pond in Rivertown Junction are quite lovely for a background as is the giant tree of The Plaza at Wilderness Pass. If you want Dollywood's most famous guest from the North Pole in your picture, head to Santa's Workshop in Country Fair.

ADVENTURES IN IMAGINATION

While traveling down Showstreet and away from the bakery, you will see a cobblestone bridge on your right before you get to the Front Porch Cafe. This bridge recrosses the same stream you initially passed when you entered the park. Ahead of you is Dolly's next land: Adventures in Imagination. While the rest of the park represents Dolly's outside world, this land represents what's going on inside. Think of this area as the soul of Dollywood.

Added in 1996, this land was originally called "Dollywood Boulevard" and carried a classic Hollywood theme. However, after a few years the area went through a transformation. No official word was given by park administration, but I suspect they were looking for a new place to locate Dolly's Museum, which had overgrown its abode over in The Village. Since Dolly's life and career contains so much more than Hollywood, the entire land was rethemed and is now, decidedly, the most Dollyesque area of Dollywood.

Adventures in Imagination is the second land that does not have any rides. But, if you are a fan of thrill rides, don't worry. I assure you that many fantastic rides are located toward the back of the park. Shops and theaters dominate the front lands as most of the large modern coasters were added later and required space farther back from the entrance. There is one exception, and you may see the world's fastest wooden coaster launching in the near distance. But for right now, focus on the imagined reality right in front of you.

DREAMSONG THEATER

The large building that dominates the edge of Adventures in Imagination is the Dreamsong Theater. Originally built as a 4-D motion simulator attraction for Dollywood Boulevard, the building was renovated in 2013, transforming it into a venue for live shows.

My People, the current show at the Dreamsong Theater, is one of the best shows ever presented at the park. Some of Dolly's relatives join a live band to share pieces of her life story told through song. Using technology, Dolly joins the cast via an interactive video that laughs and sings along. Several new songs are premiered in the production along with Dolly's biggest hits.

The cast is subject to change, but usually includes Dolly's brother Randy and sister Cassie. Both are accomplished artists in their own right. Joining them are a couple cousins, nieces, and friends that share stories during the fifty-five-minute journey. Like the Von Trapp's, this is one musical family and those of you who enjoy the sound of family music will love this show. *My People* normally opens in late spring and continues to the end of the operating season.

During Smoky Mountain Christmas, a special holiday version of *My People* is presented. The first portion of the show remains the same as it tells Dolly's story. During the second portion, the cast performs holiday songs. Dolly's niece Jada Star Anderson raises the roof during a gospel-inspired rendition of "Go, Tell It on the Mountain." Another niece, Heidi Lou Parton, brings the audience to tears performing a heartfelt "Hard Candy Christmas."

Butterfly Wisdom

Look for the memorial garden along the mountain stream side of Dreamsong Theater. This garden is not marked on the park maps. Along the edge of the garden, bronze plaques memorialize the names of people who have journeyed on from Dolly's life. Some of the names are famous and you will recognize them. Other names you may not know, but rest assured they are even more important to Dolly.

DOLLY'S CLOSET

Across the plaza from the Dreamsong Theater you won't be able to miss the sparkling butterflies of Dolly's Closet. This shop has its motto, Dolly's style...your size, proudly displayed above the door. And, that is exactly what you will find inside.

You may need to wear sunglasses in here because there is a lot of bling—that's how Dolly wants it! In fact, a seamstress is on hand daily to add extra sparkle to any outfit you purchase. Seriously! Even if this type of attire isn't your normal thing, it's worth a peak inside. Who knows? You may find a sparkly sweater to wear for your next office Christmas party.

DOLLY'S HOME-ON-WHEELS

Parked in the middle of the plaza is the large tour bus that Dolly once called home as she traveled across the country. This vehicle was recently retired when Dolly bought a new one and it's fascinating to see how efficiently the small space was used.

A tour guide allows a few people at a time to board the bus. You can see Dolly's mobile kitchen, bathroom, bedroom, and closet. The guide will explain various features of the bus and give statistics about the many miles traveled. Last, a photo of your group is taken that you can purchase outside after you step down from the door.

Be advised that since only a small group is allowed on the bus at one time, the line can move quite slowly. If the bus is on your "must see" list and there is any sort of line, try coming back during popular meal times. Also, the bus may have shorter hours than the rest of the park; a sign is posted by the door with the current day's schedule.

CHASING RAINBOWS MUSEUM

Even if you've never heard of Dolly Parton, if you go all the way to Dollywood and don't visit the Chasing Rainbows Museum, I will personally haunt your dreams. Again, by purchasing this book you are legally obligated to visit the museum. Okay, that's a lie. The fact is, this is how all celebrity museums, including presidential libraries, should look. There are no depressing dingy displays and meaningless quotes plastered on the walls. Chasing Rainbows is a relevant, clean, and fun story. Please note: the museum is not open the entire operating day. Check on the bottom of the Dollywood Show Schedule for the opening hours.

As you enter the museum, a host will offer a heartfelt welcome and point you in the right direction. First, you will walk down a hall decorated with hundreds of photos of Dolly and other famous people. Remember when I said this museum was fun? While other museums of this sort would simply offer the photos, in Chasing Rainbows you can read comments that Dolly wrote with marker on the wall. Take your time and see faces you will recognize from music, television, and film.

At the end of the hall, you can take either the stairs or the elevator to the second floor. Now, you enter Dolly's attic. Again, take your time and look at some of the stuff this famous packrat has collected over her long career. Suddenly, you will hear a familiar laugh as Dolly appears right in the attic via a hologram. This portion of the museum was renovated in 2013 and the hologram is truly a marvel. Dolly will officially welcome you to the museum and explain the importance of her "dream more" philosophy.

The rest of the museum is yours to tour at leisure. As you continue on the second floor, you will see artifacts important to Dolly's Smoky Mountain upbringing. A recreated schoolroom and church give you a glimpse of what life was like. Also, right in a display case for all to see, is the very coat that inspired Dolly's immortal song "Coat of Many Colors." Please respect the museum's no-photography policy so that future visitors may also enjoy the vibrant colors of the little coat.

When you've seen the top floor, descend on the open staircase and notice the floral swing Dolly used to open each episode of her variety show in the 1970s. Now, put on your sunglasses again because you are about to see Dolly's collection of awards…there is a lot of platinum, gold, silver, brass, and bronze in this space! Plaques, records, and more Grammy's than you can count fill the shelves. Don't miss the unique design of Dolly's Kennedy Center Honor with its rainbow ribbon and gold bars.

Leave your sunglasses on for the rest of the first floor. Designer gowns featured on red carpets and their matching shoes are displayed. You can also see costumes from all of Dolly's movies and watch clips of her guest appearances on several sitcoms, including *Hannah Montana* with goddaughter Miley Cyrus.

Always being updated, the museum contains costumes and props from Dolly's recent Christmas movies. You can see the sparkly designer gowns she wore to introduce the films, as well as the "trashy get-ups" she donned when she portrayed the Painted Lady of Sevierville. In the same display is, of course, the colorful coat that a Hollywood designer created for the little actress who played young Dolly. This one glass case symbolically sums up Dolly Parton's entire career—there is a lot for all of us to learn here.

The museum includes several places to watch short films and contains a wall where you can use headphones to listen to Dolly's albums. The last display you will see contains a tribute to Dolly's philanthropy work and highlights the Imagination Library.

Exit the theater and take a right. As you leave Adventures in Imagination, take a second to turn and look at Dolly's picture above the Dreamsong Theater. This land is unique to Dollywood and you won't find one like it anywhere else. Even without Dolly, Adventures in Imagination represents the best of humanity: imagination, hard work, and the power of dreaming. When you are ready, continue toward the sounds of rock-n-roll and screaming teenagers. The teenagers may be screaming for a roller coaster, and not for Elvis, but there will be no doubt that you have entered Jukebox Junction.

JUKEBOX JUNCTION

Even though parts of Dolly Parton aren't as old as others, she still grew up in the 1950s. The influence this decade had on Dolly is evident in the recreated 50s main street called Jukebox Junction. This section of the park was added in 1995 and is well themed to the era it represents. Vintage cars are often parked here and it's fun to hear the appropriate music throughout the area.

Take some time to wonder past the fantasy realness of the shop windows along the street. The items for sale in these fantasy shops look new, but they are actually carefully selected antiques.

All of the fantasy names for these shops have some sort of special place in Dolly's life. For example, Judy, of Judy's Luggage & Millinery Shop, refers to Dolly's lifelong friend Judy Ogle. Cas Walker's Super Market was a real grocery store in Knoxville where a very young Dolly Parton once sang on a radio show.

PINES THEATER

As with the previous two lands, the largest building in Jukebox Junction is also a theater. The Pines Theater is designed after a real theater Dolly visited while growing up in Sevierville. This is the fourth theater in Dollywood capable of producing large productions with Broadway-style sets.

During the spring, summer, and fall the theater presents *Dreamland Drive-In*. This production show is about an hour long and features a large talented cast as they perform hits of the 50s and 60s. There is a bit of a story and a nice set that reflects the drive-in movie theater where the action happens. However, the period costumes are the most fun. Part of the show is about a radio station broadcasting from the drive-in. Notice that the station is WDLY AM1430. WDLY was a real radio station Dolly purchased in 1990 to broadcast live from Dollywood. The country music station operated under the slogan, "We're Dolly's station." However, the station was never able to grab a large enough piece of the local market and Dolly sold it in 2000.

The show at the Pines for Smoky Mountain Christmas is called *'Twas the Night Before Christmas*. Contrary to the title, the show's story does not revolve around the famous Christmas poem, although portions of it are recited. Once again, this is a full-stage production with sets and lavish Christmas costumes. The story, and all the live music, tells of a family's attempts to be together for Christmas against some impossible odds. Yes, it's sappy. Yes, it's predictable. But it's Christmas and this show is exactly what you want at that time of year. Plus, the live music is top-notch and something that is hard to find when you get back home.

'Twas the Night Before Christmas isn't as popular as the other Christmas shows in the park, still, be in line at least forty-five minutes before showtime. On days during the holidays when the park is extremely popular, hosts may distribute vouchers for the show so that you don't have to wait in a multi-hour line.

RED'S DRIVE-IN

So, you won't actually be able to drive in to Red's since it's a theme park and driving on the themed streets isn't exactly allowed. But, you can enjoy some of the cars parked outside that give you the feeling you are stepping back in time. My mom, born the same year as Dolly, loves this restaurant and it's always a "must-do" when we visit the park with her.

Red's serves hamburgers, hotdogs, and fries. Of course, there are the mandatory milk shakes that all 1950s diners have to offer. If you are hungry from all the walking you are doing around the park, the Big Bopper is a half-pound burger and the Jukebox Special is a half-pound bacon cheeseburger. Red's also offers grilled chicken and vegetarian burgers if you are not quite ready for that much meat. The hosts at Red's dress appropriately for the theme and it's generally a fun place to eat. There are many tables available, both inside and out. In cooler weather the outdoor tables are heated.

Look for the wall inside the restaurant that describes Dolly's famous feud with Elvis Presley over the song *I Will Always Love You*.

Butterfly Wisdom

Dollywood has an app that you can download from the Apple App Store and Google Play. The app is free and is a quick way to check park hours. You may also find the map feature useful. Even though I love technology, I still like using a paper map because it's quicker to grab and I can write on it.

You can buy single-day tickets via the app and access some games based on Dollywood rides. There are suggested itineraries for various types of guests, like thrill seekers and parents with young children, but it's probably easier just to ask your kids what they want to do. Reservation information for both Dollywood's DreamMore Resort and Dollywood's Smoky Mountain Cabins can be found on the app.

The most useful features are the abilities to check ride wait times and theater showtimes. The app will also inform you if a ride is temporarily closed for weather or shut down all day.

GEM TONES

Right outside Red's Drive-In you can catch the short performances of the Gem Tones—Dollywood's resident 1950s quintet. Watch and listen as the cheerleader, jock, nerd, and others bring the best harmonies of the era to life. The Gem Tones are listed on the Dollywood show schedule. Sometimes the group performs inside the drive-in, so make sure to find them in the correct location.

During Dollywood's Smoky Mountain Christmas, the Gem Tones become the MistleTones. They perform holiday standards, with fine tight harmonies, inside the gazebo on Showstreet.

LIGHTNING ROD

The first major thrill ride on our tour, and the newest addition to Dollywood's already impressive coaster collection, Lightning Rod represents everything the park does right: theming, appeal, and design.

Do you remember that scene in the movie *Grease* when the T-Birds overhaul a car and race it through a Los Angeles spillway? That's the idea behind Lightning Rod's theme and explains why it fits so well in Jukebox Junction. Although it's not recommended that you drag race down the Parkway—the traffic would never allow for it anyway—now you can feel the wind in your slicked-back hair inside Dollywood. The coaster itself looks like a hot rod that's on fire. And it should—it's the fastest wooden roller coaster in the world.

Despite the nostalgic theming, Lightning Rod is more about the future than the past. Dollywood is smart when it comes to strategic planning, and the planners know what appeals to the future. For example, my oldest nephew is sixteen years old. He knows that Dolly Parton is a singer, and that's about it. But he still loves Dollywood. Why does an urban kid from cosmopolitan Minneapolis love the same rural theme park that his great-grandparents frequented? Simple—he loves the rides.

Lightning Rod is the world's fastest wooden roller coaster. It's also the world's only wooden launch coaster that launches riders up the initial twenty-story climb in just a few seconds. The coaster features no less than twelve moments when the rider feels weightless. A ninety-degree banked turn puts riders completely on their sides.

Most coasters offer a different, slightly more thrilling, ride at night. However, that statement is magnified one-hundred fold with Lightning Rod. This coaster is completely different at night because there are no lights back in the foothills to illuminate… well…anything. While I use "fantastically thrilling" to describe Lightning Rod during the day, I'll use "unbelievably terrifying" to describe it at night. I can handle it maybe one time each night—then I remember what it's like and swear I'll never do it again. If you have a TimeSaver pass, save your one ride on Lightning Rod until it is pitch dark.

This coaster is stunning and quite hard to describe. It is a fantastic example of Dollywood using the natural terrain to its advantage. That first twenty-story climb? An actual Smoky Mountain foothill that's been there since way before Rebel Railroad came to town. In fact, because of that foothill, much of Lightning Rod is not visible to those inside the park.

Speaking to Dollywood's use of nature, because Lightning Rod extends out from the park and into the forest, great care was taken to protect the environment during construction. Dollywood's obsession with its trees costs it a lot of money because not one tree was chopped down—they were transplanted.

Have you ever driven past a construction site and noticed all sort of trash blowing around? Not just construction trash, but fast-food wrappers and cans? It's frustrating, but you can hardly blame the workers for not wanting to stop a multimillion-dollar project in order to throw away a Big Mac wrapper. At Dollywood, management took the matter into its own hands. The park designated the construction zone litter-free and made sure trash bins were placed throughout the area. Also, park employees donned hard hats and cleaned litter from the site each day. Sometimes the smallest and easily attainable goals make the biggest difference.

There is one special note that may need to be considered. Lightning Rod uses a unique restrain system to keep riders safely in their seats. There aren't any shoulder harnesses, instead, large braces secure riders' legs and torsos. Remember, it is the fastest wooden coaster on the planet. Consequently, larger riders will not be able to ride. There is a test seat at the entrance to the line. If you are in any doubt that you will fit—use the test seat before getting into line. The size limit of Lightning Road is considerably smaller than other coasters. I've seen lots of people turned away after an hour wait because the safety system would not latch.

Lightning Rod is a triumph of theme, appeal, and design. With a nod to the past, it launches into the future while ensuring that all ages can find something to love about Dollywood.

COASTER FACTS: LIGHTNING ROD

Length:	3,800 feet
Tallest Drop:	165 feet
Max Speed:	73 mph
Total Airtime Moments:	12

ROCKIN' ROADWAY

Here, all ages can enjoy driving and/or riding in a replica 1950s automobile. I've seen some Cadillac, Corvettes, and even Thunderbirds come around the bend of the track. The cars look small, but they are easier to get into than you might imagine.

The best part of this ride is the nicely themed area your car drives through. It's always fun to pass the vintage billboards and signs. Okay, if you're a teenager or older, this ride is not going to blow your mind or change your life. But remember that for kids, driving a car is a big deal and this ride can be immensely fun for the whole family. Do your little brother or sister a favor and take them on the Rockin' Roadway.

Now, step away from the poodle skirts and cross back over the mountain stream on either side of Red's Drive-In. Jukebox Junction is the most saccharine and nostalgic land in Dollywood; I say this with the best intention. This area is what you want it to be. Does it exactly represent life in the 1950s? Of course not...it's still a theme park with the goal of entertainment. Push aside thoughts of the Cold War and the approaching domestic turmoil of the 1960s. Be glad that you can enjoy this era as a snapshot.

Regardless of which bridge you used to cross the stream, you will find yourself in Rivertown Junction.

RIVERTOWN JUNCTION

Rivertown Junction is that town that was nestled way back in the mountains. I imagine it was harder to get to because it lacked a railroad station. There are no posh Showstreet-type houses here and the residents had to entertain themselves. The kids of the town use the river as their source of adventure and fun. The folks of Rivertown Junction know Southern cooking better than their neighbors in Jukebox Junction or the nearby Village, and their restaurants reflect that.

MARKET SQUARE

The main entrance to Rivertown Junction is through Market Square. You can easily see, smell, and hear this unique archway that is built to look like an open-air market for the residents of Rivertown. Market Square is really a collection of several quick-service eateries, including some that use enormous skillets to cook their menu items. The skillets are five feet in diameter and the sizzle they create can be heard and deliciously smelled.

Fresh vegetables and meats are prepared and served mainly as sandwiches. The highlight of the skillets are the smoked sausages that taste as good as they smell. In addition to the skillets, small shacks in Market Square serve salads, wraps, smoothies, and shave ice. These shacks change their offerings during spring's Festival of Nations. During this festival a multitude of international snacks is served. (My personal favorite is always whatever Japan is offering.)

Nearby, there are areas with tables and umbrellas—especially in the plaza near the TimeSaver Reservation Center.

Butterfly Wisdom

Since this is the first quick-service type restaurant I've written about, it's a good time to explain the Dollywood refillable mugs. You can purchase a large plastic covered mug that is designed with the year and pictures of a new attraction. The mugs can be bought and refilled at most dining locations in the park. The initial purchase of one mug is $14.99, two mugs for $19.99, three are $24.99 and four will cost you $29.99. A fountain drink refill for the mug costs $.99 and you can get it refilled with a hot or frozen beverage for $1.99. The water park has its own mug that can be refilled for free; I'll explain that in the next chapter—but these Dollywood mugs can be refilled for $.99 at Dollywood's Splash Country. Guests at Dollywood's DreamMore Resort can refill their mug for $.99 at DM Pantry. I know I sound like a broken record, but do the math and decide if it works financially for you to get one or more refillable mugs. For your reference, a medium cup of fountain soda costs $3.99.

COUNTRY COOKERS

Normally, I would not devote a separate section to a small stand that sells just one thing, however, the thing they sell is so good that it deserves a headline. Country Cookers makes the best kettle corn you are likely to eat all year. I believe it's because they sell so much of it that you are assured a fresh batch.

You can get the regular kettle corn you've seen before, or a multi-colored version that tastes the same, but is somehow more fun to eat. Also, Country Cookers makes a version with Splenda that is perfect for those watching their intake of refined sugar. The popcorn can be purchased in bags of various sizes or a refillable bucket.

SMOKY MOUNTAIN RIVER RAMPAGE

If you can, try to ignore the smells of kettle corn and the skillets as you walk toward the large pond in the middle of Rivertown Junction. As you get closer, you will notice the familiar scent of funnel cakes from Crossroads Funnel Cakes. As you have noticed, Rivertown is a feast for the nose!

The pond is a lovely spot for a photo and a nice place to sit and relax. However, the serenity is occasionally interrupted by nearby screams. Walk along the pond and you will soon see the raging stream that is Smoky Mountain River Rampage. The riders aren't screaming in fear of the funnel cakes, they're screaming because they just got soaking wet!

Smoky Mountain River Rampage is a traditional river raft ride that most theme parks offer. However, because of the real mountain terrain and nearby streams, Dollywood's version is more immersive. Groups of six ride on large rafts through the rapids and waterfalls of a mountain river. At one point in the ride, you float through an old mill that adds a bit of excitement.

Heed the warnings, because you probably will get very wet. Depending upon the weather, you might really like the refreshing splash of this ride! Also, if you've ridden once, you might as well ride again because you can't get any wetter than soaked. If your whole party is riding and you have items you want to keep dry, there are lockers at the entrance for storage. This ride, and other water rides at Dollywood, do not operate during Smoky Mountain Christmas.

Butterfly Wisdom

If you have children, or especially teenagers in your group, you will constantly be begged to ride Smoky Mountain River Rampage with them. It's a law of the theme park universe that kids love seeing their parents and grandparents get soaked on a raft ride. Actually, these types of water rides can be a ton of fun—until you have to spend the next four hours walking around in wet clothes.

At your local dollar store, and online, you can find very cheap rain ponchos. These ponchos are cheap in both price and quality; they are hardly thicker than plastic food wrap. Because they are so thinly made, they are folded in compact sleeves that can easily be thrown in any bag. While I'd never want to rely on one of these in a real rainstorm, they are perfect for theme park raft rides. And since they normally cost less than a dollar, you can dispose of them after the kids have had a good laugh at you.

MOUNTAIN LAUREL HOME

As you exit the River Rampage and squish your way down the path, head back to the serene pond and enter the shop that looks like a small mill. This is my favorite store in Dollywood because the merchandise is displayed creatively and neatly beside a rotating waterwheel. Mountain Laurel HOME sells things for gardeners and people who love small outdoor critters. You will not find traditional theme park merchandise in this shop. Instead, there are sections devoted to squirrels, owls, bunnies, and all sorts of flowers and birds. Even if you aren't into this sort of thing, still go inside and be amazed at all the things they can make with squirrels on them!

The best theme parks are the ones that devote attention to small details. Dollywood is no exception and the Mountain Laurel HOME is an excellent example of how even a shop changes displays to match the current season.

AUNT GRANNY'S BUFFET

This is my favorite place to eat in the park. For me, Aunt Granny's is the perfect blend of Southern food and ambience. I can't tell what I like better: the cornbread or the large windows that overlook the pond of Rivertown Junction.

First, the name. Aunt Granny is a title Dolly gave herself when her grandnieces and nephews were at a loss of who she was. She wasn't their aunt, and wasn't their grandma...she was Aunt Granny. If you are lucky enough to be passing by at opening time, you will see a Dollywood host dressed as Aunt Granny as she rings a giant dinner bell on the porch. (She'll be dressed not as Dolly Parton as Aunt Granny, but rather what you'd expect an Aunt Granny to look like.)

Here, you can try many of Dolly's Southern recipes in a buffet that includes beverages. Chicken, beef, and fish are served along with mashed potatoes, biscuits, and unbelievable macaroni and cheese. A full salad bar is available with fresh fruits and vegetables. Perhaps the best part of Aunt Granny's is the separate kids buffet. Build-your-own tacos and the cutest hot dogs you'll ever see are served on this pint-sized buffet. Even if you don't have kids with you, still feel free to visit the kid's buffet—I always do! End your meal at the dessert bar with a piece of pie, cake, or fresh banana pudding.

During Smoky Mountain Christmas, a special buffet is offered. While most of the items remain the same, you will find the additions of roast turkey and pumpkin pie.

UPPER RIVERTOWN JUNCTION SHOPS

You probably aren't used to eating this much food at a theme park, especially if it's a hot day. So, take your time and enjoy the surroundings. If you need a break to meander before doing anything too strenuous, there are two shops around the back of Aunt Granny's; just climb the slightly steep hill.

The Mountain Blown Glass Factory is located up the hill behind the buffet. Next to the ovens where artists are working with molten glass, there is a large store full of beautiful creations. During Smoky Mountain Christmas you can make your own glass ornament.

Also back on this hill you will notice a shop that looks like a small church—it's hard to miss because its guarded by two enormous nutcrackers. This is the Smoky Mountain Christmas Cottage and, yes, it's open all year around. It's a beautiful shop that deserves a look even if you don't plan on purchasing anything. Inside, you'll find trees full of colorful ornaments, many with a Smoky Mountain theme. There is always Christmas music playing inside this shop. On a very hot and humid day, the cottage's air-conditioning and holiday melodies are a welcome respite.

DOLLY'S TENNESSEE MOUNTAIN HOME

As you're strolling back down the hill into Rivertown Junction, you won't be able to miss the large sign describing the small home where Dolly grew up. Then, get in line and have a glimpse at a full-scale reproduction of the mountain cabin that housed all those Partons. The building may be a replica, but most of the items displayed inside, and behind glass, are the real things used by the people of the time. It will be difficult for kids in your group to relate to the type of decor that adorned Dolly's childhood walls.

Even if there is a line, once you get to the actual structure there is plenty of space in the walkway so you can take your time and notice all the interesting things. The home is not as well done as the museum, so I'm not making it mandatory that you see it. But if you want to show your kids what the American Dream looks like, this is about as good a place as any to start.

Butterfly Wisdom

Face the entrance to Dolly's old house and look to your right. You will see a "house" that contains a restaurant called Dogs N Taters. The first floor of this building was originally the Apple Jack Sandwich Shop, named after one of Dolly's hit songs. Now, look at the side of the building facing the train tracks and you will notice a set of wooden steps ascending to a door on the outside of the second floor. At one time, this was the door to Dolly's private apartment inside the park.

The decor of the apartment remains a mystery, but there was an elaborate bed that Dolly donated to a charity auction a few years ago. Nobody, outside of those closest to her, knows how much the apartment was used. There were numerous times over the years when Dolly made appearances on consecutive days at the park; we can assume she occupied the apartment on those occasions. However, as Dollywood gained attendance and began to expand its hours, it became impractical—and downright dangerous—for Dolly to sneak through the park to her apartment. A couple of years ago, Dolly purchased a new bus that she uses as her home while visiting the Smoky Mountains.

Even though the apartment is no longer in use, I love the idea of Dolly sitting up there in her pajamas as she watched guests mulling around Rivertown Junction. I'm not sure if that ever happened, but each time I pass this structure, I look up at the window and smile—just in case.

BACK PORCH THEATER

Dolly's Tennessee Mountain Home is kind of like the TARDIS on the British show *Dr. Who*: it's much bigger on the other side! Dolly's home, and all the shops adjacent to it, are really the back facade of a giant outdoor theater. Walk around and see for yourself.

The Back Porch Theater is the place for authentic mountain music at Dollywood. Even when the weather is not cooperating, the theater is covered and has ceiling fans that provide a gentle breeze. If you like bluegrass, then plant yourself on a seat and stay for the entire afternoon. (Get some kettle corn first.)

The Smoky Mountain String Band is featured during most of the Dollywood operating season. This ensemble is entertaining and interesting. Their sets usually last around thirty minutes, but they tend to change up the songs if you want to hear more than one set. During the National Gospel and Harvest Festival, this venue becomes host to many of the guest artists.

For Smoky Mountain Christmas, an additional show provides even more live music at the Back Porch Theater. The show, *Appalachian Christmas*, has a more authentic mountain sound than the shows over in Showstreet. That doesn't mean it's any better or worse, just that Showstreet features production shows and every note at the Back Porch is acoustic. Sometimes you want to see a big Christmas spectacular, and sometimes you just want to hear a woman with a dulcimer sing a simple "Silent Night"—at Dollywood you can do both!

The show times for all performances at the Back Porch Theater are printed in the *This Week at Dollywood* guide.

BACK PORCH SHOPS AND SNACKS

Surrounding the seating area of the Back Porch Theater are a couple of shops and a great place for a quick snack.

Back Porch Concessions is located toward the back of the audience and near the path coming down from Mountain Blown Glass.

As the name implies, you can grab some snacks that come freshly baked from the bakery in Showstreet. Back Porch Concessions also offers a selection of hot and cold beverages. If you've been to a Disney Park anywhere on the planet, you've seen pretzels in the shape of Mickey Mouse. Here, you can purchase a pretzel in the shape of a butterfly!

On the Aunt Granny's side of the theater you will find Rivertown Trading. Here is where the womenfolk of Rivertown Junction do their fancier shopping. Sundresses, handbags, hats and jewelry line the shelves. This is a more practical alternative to the bedazzled garments of Dolly's Closet.

On the opposite side of the theater, Tin Sign Shoppe will give you a taste of what you will see when you eventually venture into Craftsman's Valley. Artisans at the slate works paint intricate scenes on actual slate roof tiles. Most of the paintings depict the Smoky Mountains at various times throughout the year. These works of art make an excellent remembrance of your time in the mountains.

DOGS N TATERS

Across the path from Tin Sign Shoppe lies another quick-service dining option. Dogs N Taters offers...well...dogs and taters. Foot-long corn dogs are the most popular menu item, but there are also chili cheese dogs. You know those spiral-cut potatoes that are fried and served at every fair in the United States? Well, they were invented right here at Dollywood! A Dollywood host had the idea of putting a potato in an apple peeler and then threw the whole thing in the fryer. You're going to do a lot of walking at Dollywood, so you might as well go ahead and indulge.

It's time to leave the good people of Rivertown Junction and journey on. Climb the embankment beside Dogs N Taters. If the railroad bars are down, you'll have to wait for the train. Otherwise, go ahead and cross the tracks. Technically, you're now in The Village. However, the sight of a country fair in the distance suddenly distracts us. So, let's explore the fair first and then head back into the railroad town. Continue alongside the tracks and down the hill until you see the whirls, twirls, and colorful sights of Country Fair.

COUNTRY FAIR

The folks of Rivertown Junction and The Village are in luck because a nice country fair has come to the vacant lot in the railroad bend. This is the place were kids of all ages can spin and ride in vehicles of all kinds of animal shapes. Of course, there are some tasty fair treats nearby and prizes to be won at the games of skill.

Actually, I really like what Dollywood has done with Country Fair. "Flat ride" is an industry term for any ride that's not a coaster, kiddie-ride, or water-ride. Bumper-cars, scramblers, swings, and tilt-a-whirls are all considered flat rides. Most other theme parks realize they have to include these popular rides, but they don't always know what to do with them. You will often see the flat rides scattered around and tucked into tight places all over an entire park. At Dollywood, most of these rides are located in Country Fair; it makes for a very nice themed experience. (And before I forget, don't worry that there isn't a kiddie coaster in Country Fair—there is a brand-spanking new one on the other side of the park.)

My twelve-year-old nephew loves the flat rides and here he can hop from one to the other without having to cross entire lands. Country Fair also includes a number of kiddie-rides for little sisters and brothers to occupy themselves. You probably need a break from me at this point, so I've asked my nephew Jordan to describe the rides of Country Fair for you.

THE SCRAMBLER

"I love the Scrambler. It's got like a nice Tennessee painting on it. It's a fun ride. When you're on it, it looks like you're going to run into a wall, but then you don't! It's fun for any age person to go on. Even a teenager."

PIGGY PARADE

"It's supposed to be that you are riding in a pig. Going around in circles, very fun and relaxing for kids. It's a nice place to take pictures of your kids while they're riding around in pigs. The kids will love it because of the scarecrow in the middle. You're riding on pigs, so you have to love it."

LUCKY DUCKY

"Fun for little kids, like Piggy Parade. But, this one is ducks. Parents will know that the kids are safe because it is nice and relaxing. To be honest, this ride is a little young for me. I mean, I probably wouldn't be caught dead on it and might not even fit inside the duck. But lots of little kids love the ducks and the pigs at Dollywood."

THE AMAZING FLYING ELEPHANTS

"Is a fun amazing ride for a kid and parents. It's good because you can pick your height. So, if you're scared of going high you can not go high. It's fun for kids because it gives them something to look at. Another amazing thing is that it's relaxing and I bet they will enjoy going up and down. One time I said that this ride was the same as the Dumbo ride at Disneyland. Then my uncle started talking about something called 'copyright' and told me that Mickey Mouse doesn't need to know about this ride at Dollywood.

2020 DOLLYWOOD AND BEYOND!

BUSY BEES

"Is a lot like Lucky Duck and Piggy Parade, but it's bees. There's a beehive. What kids will really love is noticing that you feel like you are driving an actual bee. I would never ride this ride, not because it's for little kids, but because I've been stung by a lot of bees. Seriously, I always seem to be the one to get stung—I just got stung last week at the zoo! The good thing is that I know I'm not allergic to bee stings, if I was I'd be dead by now."

SHOOTING STAR

"This small dropping ride is built for fun. It's all right for kids, but if they have a fear of heights they should not go on it. You will be up in the sun, so wear sunscreen. You can see the Smoky Mountains. It's also fun and not too boring for grown ups. This is one of those rides that a whole family can go on together."

LEMON TWIST

"Is just like the teacup ride at Disneyland. You're like in a teacup. It's fun for all ages when you spin really fast. There is something like a teapot in the middle. You might throw up. My uncle said that this is another ride that Mickey Mouse doesn't need to know about."

DEMOLITION DERBY

"These cars are like going around in a circle and crash into other drivers. Lots of theme parks call this ride the 'bumper cars.' This is not a relaxing ride because people are crashing at you. You can drive uncontrollably and get some anger out of you. It's good to go on these cars if you're mad at your brother. Make sure to buckle up on it and follow all the safety rules."

MICHAEL FRIDGEN

THE WALZING SWINGER

"Very fun thing to swing while spinning in circles. You can notice a lot of stuff when you go around. Very great for adults and kids. Fun moving at a very high speed. Fun for parents to watch. It's just a lot of fun."

SKY RIDER

"This ride is a lot like the swings, but a little slower. But it does go much higher. It's fun to look around and see the other parts of the park. You're not moving very fast and you can get sunburn. If you have a fear of heights, you should not go on it. There are some amazing views."

DIZZY DISC

"This up and down spinning fast ride is a blast. Little kids, I don't think, should go on this because they will probably throw up. Do not go on this ride right after lunch. There is a thing that squishes your back, but it's a very smooth ride. You will lose your stomach a lot and that can be fun if you're used to it. This might be a good ride for kids to try before they try a real roller coaster."

Thanks, Nephew. I'll take the reins back from here.

GRANDSTAND CAFE AND MIDWAY MARKET

There are two places to eat in the Country Fair. Grandstand Cafe serves more substantial meals like hamburgers, hotdogs, and fried chicken sandwiches. Their chili-cheese fries are always piled high, just as they should be at the fair. However, I'm often surprised at the quality of the salads offered at the Grandstand Cafe. If you're in the mood for something light and fresh, the strawberry spinach salad might be the best thing you see all day.

2020 DOLLYWOOD AND BEYOND!

Across the path you can find Midway Market. This eatery offers more of the traditional fair food: cotton candy, cookies, popcorn, etc... If it's summer and you want something cold, cross back to the Grandstand Cafe side and find Country Fair Soft Serve next to the cafe.

There is a large seating area in the middle of Country Fair that is partly shielded from the sun. This area also includes a portion that is covered with imitation grass. Many families enjoy relaxing in this space.

GAMES

Spending a lot of money and winning an outrageously large stuffed animal is a staple of the Great American Fair. You won't be disappointed because Dollywood offers two areas for this type of experience. One is here in Country Fair and the other is at the very far end of Craftsman's Valley. The prizes, and some of the actual games, change frequently, so I won't describe them here. But, rest assured, you will have plenty of opportunities to win something that will take an extra seat on the parking lot tram.

CELEBRATION HALL AND BLUE RIBBON PAVILION

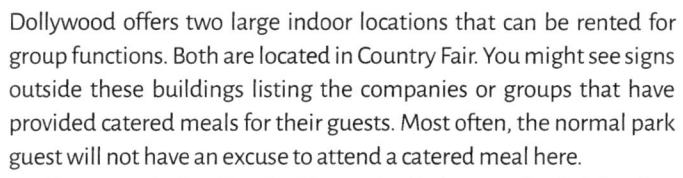

Dollywood offers two large indoor locations that can be rented for group functions. Both are located in Country Fair. You might see signs outside these buildings listing the companies or groups that have provided catered meals for their guests. Most often, the normal park guest will not have an excuse to attend a catered meal here.

However, during Smoky Mountain Christmas the Celebration Hall becomes a major attraction. Santa's Workshop is located inside the hall during this special event. Themed like a store for enormous toys, Santa's Workshop makes it possible to explore oversized versions of famous gifts. The workshop is very interactive and there is plenty of twinkling and jingling going on. Inside

Kringle Kids Shopping Mall, kids can find inexpensive gifts for their siblings and parents. There is a special mailbox that ensures letters are delivered directly to the North Pole. And, of course, a visit to Santa's Workshop provides a chance to sit and talk with Santa himself. Always go into Santa's Workshop, even if you don't have any kids with you. Most of us can use the extra jolt of Christmas cheer this place provides.

While jumping from ride to ride and making the most of your visit to Country Fair, you might suddenly see a huge locomotive circle the rides and the backside of Celebration Hall. If you don't see it, you will surely hear it. This is the Dollywood Express letting you know that the train is getting close to its station up in The Village. You don't want to risk missing the train, so head up the hill.

THE VILLAGE

I imagine the merchants of Showstreet were quite upset to learn that the train was not going to make a stop on their street of shops. But the mountain topography dictated where the one and only station could be and a little village sprang up around it. The Village is the birthplace of Dollywood and the oldest land in the park. In fact, it's the only place that has been part of Rebel Railroad, Goldrush Junction, Silver Dollar City, and present-day Dollywood.

As you climb out of Country Fair near the train crossing, notice the security and first-aid building on your left. Hopefully, you will not need to see inside either of these facilities, but if you need them, they are staffed during all park hours.

PAPAW'S ROADSIDE COUNTRY MARKET

At the beginning of The Village is an interesting place with a strangely delicious product. PaPaw's Roadside Country Market offer beverages and bananas. But not just the regular 'ole grocery store bananas—these are frozen and come in several varieties.

You can get them covered in chocolate, nuts, sprinkles, and chocolate sprinkles (that's 'jimmies' for those of you from Philadelphia and New Jersey). These frozen treats are surprisingly refreshing on a hot day.

OLD TIME FLASHBULB PHOTOS

The first large building of the main part of The Village is a photo studio where families can pretend to be bank robbers or saloon patrons. You will find a lot of these old time photography studios in Gatlinburg and on Parkway in Pigeon Forge. Flashbulb Photos at Dollywood will be more expensive than those off-site, but the props and costumes here are generally in better shape and cleaner.

VICTORIA'S PIZZA

Most of the residents of the Smoky Mountains are descended from English, Irish, or Welsh ancestors. Well, an Italian family must have snuck in at some point and opened a pizza restaurant across from the train station. Pizza with all kinds of toppings is made fresh, as are the warm bread sticks. Victoria's is another place where you can get a good salad.

During Smoky Mountain Christmas, the menu changes slightly when the restaurant serves warm chili in a bread bowl and some very fine pasta.

TEMPLE'S MERCANTILE

Temple's was a real store in Sevierville and now you can visit their location right in The Village. This mercantile stocks all sorts of Dollywood souvenirs, many of which can also be found in the Dollywood Emporium. However, due to its proximity to the train station, Temple's has a large selection of train-related toys, clothing, and stuffed animals. Much of the train merchandise is only found here, so purchase them and use package pick-up if you like.

On the other side of the shop, opposite the train merchandise, is a large collection of dolls for purchase. Frankly, I find many of them to be a bit creepy—but to each her own!

VILLAGE CAROUSEL

No matter what theme park you're at, you should always ride the carousel. You just should. Dollywood's beautiful carousel features many horses, but also a variety of other animals. Ostrich, rooster, dragon, zebra...take your pick. There is a pig that seems to be very popular. But, make sure to keep your eyes peeled. As the animals spin, you just might see the lead horse with its beautiful blond hair flying out in the wind. What's the official park name of that horse? Dolly, of course! (I always try to ride that horse. I once lied to by niece and told her that the zebra was way cooler than the horse so that she wouldn't steal it from me.)

HEARTSONG THEATER

Originally the Gaslight Theater, this venue was transformed in the mid-1990s into an immersive environment dubbed "Natur-round." You'll see what I mean when you enter the theater and see its many large trees stretching up into darkness. You won't see any walls here, just trees, rocks, and relaxing waterfalls. Get here early and sit in the air-conditioned comfort of the padded benches. Listen to the real flowing water and faux crickets. Look for the fireflies.

This theater is home to *Heartsong: The Movie*. Check the schedule for show times, as the twenty-minute film doesn't usually show too often. *Heartsong* is Dolly's tribute to the mountains and people of her childhood. While *My People* at the Dreamsong Theater is quite Dolly-centric, this film includes Dolly more as narrator because the mountains are the true stars. For the first few years of its operation, *Heartsong* was an immersive film. When leaves fell in the film, they also really fell from the ceiling and branches above. When it rained in the film, it rained on you. Beautiful butterflies flew around while a young girl on the screen explored a meadow. However, in recent years the interactive portions of the experience have disappeared. While not as captivating as it once was, the film is still a nice way to see impressive footage of the mountains and their many moods.

During summer, when the park is filled with children, Heartsong Theater is home to a daytime troop of repertory actors: the Penguin Players of the Imagination Library Playhouse. Three children's books are brought to life each summer by the players sponsored by Penguin Books. Each show is a complete mini-musical with original songs Dolly Parton composes specifically for that summer's repertoire. A lot of work goes into these shows and the talented singers are enthusiastic for each performance. I'm always impressed with the creativity involved in crafting the intricate sets that are used on this rather small stage. The books from the shows are available to purchase at Temple's Warehouse. There are many hard-working musicians at Dollywood, but none more than the Penguin Players that sing, play multiple characters, and change costumes probably a million times each summer.

COSTNER AND SONS MAGIC SHOP

One of the older buildings, this magic store predates Dollywood. The shop sells the usual fare of magic stores and these items are not available at the Dollywood Emporium. Outside Costner and Sons is a small covered stage with places to sit and watch a short magic show. These shows are generally not scheduled and usually begin when passengers are unloading from the nearby train station.

DOLLYWOOD EXPRESS

I'd like you to see the museum, ride the carousel, see a show, and get something Southern to eat. But, if you literally have only one hour at Dollywood and can do only one thing...it has to be the Dollywood Express. No other major theme park offers this level of immersive train experience, probably because this full-scale train is real—with steam, whistles, and heavy wheels. I can't tell if it's a coveted position or not, but some Dollywood host has to hand shovel coal into the 110-ton steam engine as you make a thirty-minute journey. They have to do this several times a day, each day during the operating season. The engine requires 2 tons of coal and four thousand gallons of water daily. (In 2019 Dollywood hired its first female coal stoker!)

You will actually leave the park during your ride and head up into the hills. The views of the mountains from the apex of the track are stunning—no matter what time of year you take the trip. Also at the top, the engineer will play a tune with the steam whistle. As the train makes a curve to head back to Dollywood, you can get a great photo of the steaming engine if you are sitting toward the back.

Dollywood owns and operates two of these vintage locomotives: Klondike Katie and Cinderella. The conductor will usually announce which engine you are riding. Every morning, it takes three hours for specialized train mechanics to prepare the locomotive for that day's journeys—this is truly a labor of love as there are not many places left where these people can practice their craft. As you might imagine, obtaining parts for these historic engines is impossible. At the Dollywood Train Shop, in the green building near the far side of Country Fair, entire engines can be built and rebuilt. What if a metal part breaks and a replacement cannot be found? No worries—Dollywood has its own blacksmith for such an occasion.

Another universal rule of all theme parks: if you are riding a train you must wave to those you pass. This will feel natural for you, as the experience is so immersive you really feel like you are leaving your small town for a trip of some length. On the journey, a guide will explain the special historical significance of Dollywood's vintage engine and its service to the United States.

There is one small negative to the experience. Remember, this is a real steam engine that burns real coal and sends real soot into the air. As you ride, you will probably find a very small speck or two of soot on your clothes and skin. Don't worry or panic—the soot will fall off when you move from the train. When you leave the station, the conductor will inform you that if a speck of soot gets in your eye, don't touch it and immediately tell a host when you return to the station. I've been on this train a lot and have never had it happen to me.

During Smoky Mountain Christmas, the train is decorated with Christmas lights and holiday music plays from the speakers as you relax in the foothills. Riding the rails, feeling the fresh air, and listening to your favorite carols provide additional layers of immersive magic to the experience.

Eventually, the train will enter back into Dollywood along Showstreet and you will cross the valley and circle Country Fair. Take in all the sights and sounds around as you let your feet rest.

The Dollywood Express gave you a good rest, which you need because we are only about halfway done with the park. Depart the train and walk toward the crossing, but don't cross. Look to your right and find a tunnel opening in the rock. You'll see an homage to Silver Dollar City as you enter. Walk through the tunnel and notice that even on a hot day, it's quite cool! This is a great place to extend your rest and there are several benches inside the tunnel. This tunnel, and the rock it's carved from, is actually the basement of a building that sits above. Dolly's original museum, Rags to Riches, was located in this building for several years and the tunnel served as the exit. When you leave the tunnel, look back over it and see remnants of the demolished old museum.

You are now at the very beginning of Craftsman's Valley. But, we're actually closer to Owens Farm than we are to most of the valley. So, let's take a short cut to the farm before exploring the valley crafters. Find the authentic flour mill across the path directly in front of you. Enter the mill. You may have to pinch yourself because you are not dreaming of heaven. The smell is real and belongs to Dollywood's famous cinnamon bread. Try not to salivate too long because the mill is the shortcut we're after. Go up the stairs inside the mill and exit the structure on the second floor. You've just entered Owens Farm.

OWENS FARM

Someone has to grow the wheat for the grist mill and raise the chickens to serve at Aunt Granny's. That someone is the Owens Family in their small hillside farm. Ironically, this is the only land at Dollywood that doesn't have a restaurant. But you can use the shortcut through the grist mill to get quickly to Craftsman's Valley, or take the path down into Rivertown Junction. Owens Farm contains two major thrill rides and the best toddler play areas in the park. Plus, the whole land is quite cute and themed to look like the typical family farm.

GRANNY'S GARDEN AND THE PIG PEN

Granny's Garden is a play-land of soft structures. Little Dollywood guests can roam around and tumble everywhere without fear of hurting themselves. The cute area is themed to match the farm and offers a couple slides and a tunnel. Dollywood is very safe, but it is still a theme park and you must supervise your children at all times. Guests younger than twelve must have someone older than sixteen with them.

The Pig Pen is a soft area with water jets embedded in the ground. Randomly, these jets shoot out a stream of water that delights children and terrifies adults. Kids will get wet in The Pig Pen—there is no way around it. But they will also have a fantastic time. Depending on the weather, adults may also want to get hit by a water jet. Granny's Garden is usually open the entire operating year. However, The Pig Pen is closed when cold weather approaches.

BARNSTORMER

Look for the big red barn with screams coming out of it—that's the Barnstormer. This extreme swing ride is not for the faint of heart. Themed like the daring pilots the name suggests, the ride features two giant swings that get progressively higher as they gain momentum. It's fast, tall, and riders are nearly inverted when at the top of the swing.

Often these extreme swing rides feature just one swing. Dollywood's version is more interesting because passing another swing adds an additional layer of excitement. You won't want any sort of loose item with you on this ride. There are lockers near the entrance.

LIL' PILOTS PLAYGROUND

Next to the Barnstormer, the pilot theme continues with this playground. This area offers several play structures that are more interactive, but less soft, than those of Granny's Garden. There is a large plane to explore and several slides. Make sure to check out the steel drums and play a tune that's painted on the wall in front of you.

Again, children must be supervised.

GRANNY OWENS TOYS, GADGETS, AND TOOLS

As the name suggests, this is a toy store offering items for those who enjoy Granny's Garden and Lil' Pilots Playground. Some of the stuffed animals can be found elsewhere in the park, but most of the toys and gadgets are only available here. Inside the shop you can also create your own stuffed bear. (NOTE: Granny Owens Toys, Gadgets, and Tools may or may not be open—its schedule is sporadic depending upon the season.)

It's now time for Granny to take her nap, so we must leave the farm. You can choose to take the path next to Lil' Pilots Playground, or if you need a second look at the cinnamon bread, go back into the grist mill and down the stairs. Either way, you will leave Owens Farm and enter the educational land of Craftsman's Valley.

Butterfly Wisdom

If you want the ultimate in a personalized Dollywood experience, VIP tours are available. For $199 per person, in addition to Dollywood admission, guests can access a customized and completely stress-free day of Smoky Mountain fun.

A personal tour guide accompanies VIP guests for their entire day. One meal at any of Dollywood's eateries is included in the tour price. Guests who purchase this tour also receive valet parking and delivery of all park purchases directly to your car. Also, VIP guests do not have to wait in any line.

VIP tours can be purchased online. Tours begin when the park opens in the morning and you must have at least two people in your group. If you book online, a Dollywood tour host will contact you prior to your special day in order to arrange an itinerary.

CRAFTSMAN'S VALLEY

Making something with your own hands requires skill and often makes a mess. The skilled crafters of the valley probably live in Rivertown Junction or The Village, but they work where they have space to get creative and attract crowds. Full of eateries and shops, Craftsman's Valley is also the beginning of Dollywood's string of newer thrill rides. Offering the most authentic look at mountain life, the valley contains the church and school. On top of all that, Craftsman's Valley is home to the largest bald eagle sanctuary in the entire United States.

My favorite part of this land is the mountain stream that divides the valley. Several small bridges allow you to cross from one side to the other. Above the stream, an elevated aqueduct channels water from the mountain with enough force to power the grist mill. Notice how several other shops connect to the aqueduct in order to harness the free energy of falling water.

The shadiest land in Dollywood, Craftsman's Valley has many places to sit and relax out of the sun. We will begin our journey at the valley's most recognized landmark, the grist mill, and then head all the way up to the loops of the Tennessee Tornado.

GRIST MILL

Arguably the symbolic and geographic center of Dollywood, the grist mill is fully functional and completely powered by mountain water. The mill was painstakingly built in 1982 exactly as similar mills were constructed in the nineteenth century. Wheat and corn are ground daily throughout the Dollywood operating season. The pond in front of the mill makes for one of the best photo spots in the entire park.

Some of the mill's products are immediately baked into the amazing cinnamon bread that is impossible to pass by. It's hard to find words to describe the warm, sweet, and gooey sensations of the bread. It might be good the next day if you heat it in a microwave, but I have no way of knowing that because everyone I know eats it on the spot. There are a number of chairs and a few tables adjacent to the first-floor entrance. Don't worry about utensils. Just tear the bread into chunks and pass them around. You'll want to remember that restrooms are just a bit further up the valley path to wash your hands. The only thing better at Dollywood than the bread is to get a hug from Dolly herself...and that may be only slightly better.

Aside from the famous bread, the grist mill has lots of other baked goods made on the premises. Cookies and assorted rolls are offered. If you want to try baking your own treats at home with mill flour, sacks of various types of grinds are available. Cloth sacks of pancake mix stamped with the Dollywood logo make an excellent gift. The mill also contains a large collection of Southern cookbooks for sale and a huge wall of cookie cutters. Most of the items at the grist mill are not available at the Dollywood Emporium. The sacks of fresh ground products can be heavy, so use package pick-up.

MISS SALLY'S SIT-N-SIP

Next to the grist mill, Miss Sally's is a beverage station that sells frozen drinks of all sorts. Perfect on a hot summer day, you can purchase various flavors of frozen lemonade and other types of slushy drinks. If you have the Dollywood mug, you can get a refill of any frozen drink for $1.99.

THE BATTER'S BOX AND SMOKY CREEK LEATHER AND HAT COMPANY

Two shops are immediately upstream from Miss Sally and they begin Dollywood's long parade of authentic crafters. The Batter's Box sells baseball bats that are hand turned right on the spot. In addition, you can have a crafter carve your name (or any name) into the bat. Needless to say, these make excellent gifts and cannot be purchased anywhere else in the park.

Next door, watch crafters as they hand-tool leather into all sorts of apparel, accessories, and hats. There are a lot of belts here, but unlike the belts from your local big-box store, these will last many, many years. (Unless you eat the cinnamon bread and then the genuine leather belts tend to shrink.) Go inside the shop to see the many different styles of hats from basic to ornate.

This tour of Craftsman's Valley requires a bit of meandering to cover the shops and eateries on both sides of the valley. Now, head back toward the grist mill pond and cross the path back toward the tunnel entrance to Craftsman's Valley. When you smell the delicious aroma of roasting chicken you're in the right place for our next stop.

Butterfly Wisdom

The smell of roasting chicken is a close second to the scent of the cinnamon bread. The good thing is that both are free! It doesn't cost a single penny beyond park admission to smell as much as you want at Dollywood. It also doesn't cost anything to watch and ask questions. Don't worry at all about pressure to buy things from the crafters in Craftsman's Valley. You will feel none from these folks and they will be glad you stopped by. Generally, these people are proud of their work and happy to talk about it. The blacksmith, glass blowers, wood carvers, and potters tend to get the most gawkers, but feel free to linger anywhere.

MISS LILLIAN'S CHICKEN HOUSE AND
MISS LILLIAN'S BAR-B-Q CORNER 🍽

While I like the ambiance of Aunt Granny's better, Miss Lillian's is probably the more famous and recommended buffet in Dollywood. The most apparent difference between the two is the appearance of Miss Lillian herself. The lady and hostess of the restaurant makes frequent visits throughout the day to toss you a fresh biscuit that will still be warm. She also likes to lead guests in a couple verses of well known folk songs and offers a great deal of entertainment while you dine.

Of course, chicken is the main dish on the buffet. However, it's not just fried, but also seasoned and prepared on rotisserie. There is always country-fried steak available and many southern sides. Both salad and dessert bars are ready to tempt you with fresh greens and lemon meringue pie.

During the fall, Miss Lillian's Chicken House opens early (8:30 a.m.) for a breakfast buffet. This special offering coincides with Dollywood's National Southern Gospel and Harvest Celebration. All the normal breakfast fare is available including eggs, bacon, hash browns, and the mandatory Southern biscuits and gravy. The breakfast buffet closes at 11am. Check dollywood.com for the exact dates of the festival.

Next to the Chicken House is Miss Lillian's Bar-B-Q Corner. This is a quick-service version of the buffet for those who want to eat less, spend less, and move faster. Along with the chicken selections, you can also find pork sandwiches and smoked turkey legs. If you want something healthy, the rotisserie chicken salad is fresh and amazingly tasty. If you want something not so healthy, Miss Lillian sells her blackberry cobbler at this location too.

If you don't feel like chicken and you still want to see Miss Lillian, just get aboard the Dollywood Express. Miss Lillian is usually kicking up her heels in front of her restaurant when the train passes the trestle crossing the entrance to the valley.

2020 DOLLYWOOD AND BEYOND!

VALLEY THEATER 🎵 🎄

Like the Back Porch Theater, this venue is also a covered outdoor theater. However, the theater's larger stage makes it possible to present shows with sets and larger casts. The productions are not as lavish as those in the completely indoor theaters, but you will find equally talented singers nonetheless.

During most of the year, *Country Crossroads* is the resident show at the Valley Theater. Six performers sing a large variety of country music from very old tunes to current hits. The singers are able to mix and match a nice variety of solos, duets, trios, etc...There is some choreographed dancing. Although the format of the show remains constant, the actual songs can change as performers decide to try a different number here and there.

The newest, and quickly becoming my favorite, show at Dollywood is *Songbook*. This show features the amazing duet of Jada Star and Barry J. When not performing in the *My People* show over at the Dreamsong Theater, Jada and Barry take their audiences on a tour of beautiful songs—many of which they wrote themselves. These two voices blend together so well and it's almost as if they are twin siblings. (They're not. Jada is Dolly's niece and she met Barry while performing at Dollywood.) *Songbook* is either performed here or in the Heartsongs Theater. Check *This Week at Dollywood* for the day's location. (Note: For the duo's Christmas version of *Songbook* see the description under Wings of America Theater—you'll be very glad you did.)

O Holy Night is performed during Smoky Mountain Christmas. Taking place in Biblical times, there is a bit of a story about a girl looking for an angel. Dollywood's version of a live nativity with plenty of music concludes the show.

GRANNY OGLE'S HAM AND BEANS 🍽

Granny Ogle's is one of the few nonbuffet, full-service restaurants in the park. Of course, you can order ham and beans, but also pulled pork, pot roast, and meatloaf. I highly recommend the barbecue pulled chicken. Sides include mashed potatoes, collard greens, cole slaw, and more beans. Homemade cobbler and vanilla ice cream are the required dessert at this establishment.

Granny's real-life granddaughter, Judy Ogle, is Dolly's lifelong best friend and personal assistant. You will find a few photos and references to Judy in the Chasing Rainbows Museum.

CUSTOM GLASSWORKS

Stop in to watch skilled glassworkers create amazing pieces using glass and fire. You will find jewelry for sale along with Christmas ornaments and other figurines. If you'd like a true reminder of Dollywood to bring home, make sure to check out the beautiful butterflies with their colorful glass wings.

PORK RINDS

I'm not a fan of this food item, but judging by the crowd around this stand, Dollywood must know what they're doing. There are always people waiting in line here and you will see guests walking with bags of pork rinds around the park.

STONE-PENLAND POTTERY

One of my favorite artists in the park, this is where you can see skilled hands turn mud into beauty. Members of one of the oldest families in the Smokies operate Stone-Penland Pottery. They have been crafting pottery in these hills since the mid-1800s. The clay they use is from the area, and everything is one-of-a-kind.

Take time to linger here and watch as a lump of clay is thrown on a wheel and miraculously turned into something useful. You can see the whole process, including the glazing and firing of the pieces.

What I like best about Stone-Penland is that all the products are not only beautiful, but also useful in everyday life. Mugs, kitchenware, dining place sets, pots, and candleholders fill the large shop. Some of the baking dishes are made using a process that enables them to be used in your oven at home. For a special souvenir of your time at Dollywood, check out the pieces that have butterflies carved into them.

During both the Harvest Festival and Smoky Mountain Christmas, Stone-Penland creates products with Halloween and Christmas themes. The handcrafted jack-o'-lanterns are especially nice. Needless to say, pieces from Stone-Penland make excellent gifts. Use package pick-up to protect your purchases as you enjoy the rest of Craftsman's Valley.

ROBERT F. THOMAS CHAPEL

On one cold January day, Dr. Robert F. Thomas delivered a baby girl in a small mountain home. He was paid with a sack of cornmeal. That girl grew up to be Dolly Parton, and she honored the revered doctor by naming the Dollywood chapel after him. The line between the real world and fantasy theme park is very blurry in Craftsman's Valley. This is a real church with actual services on Sundays throughout the operating season.

Even if you're not Christian, or aren't interested in attending a service, the chapel is a work of art that is nestled back in the trees. The church creates a nice environment to relax and reflect on your day.

During Smoky Mountain Christmas, the chapel is decorated nicely and has a life-size nativity placed next to it.

VALLEY WOOD CARVERS

We've completed a section of the valley, so now you can cross the stream and head back to see what you've been missing on the other side. It's easy to find the Valley Wood Carvers because they have a large porch displaying hand-carved statues.

Everything from small ornaments to full-size carousel horses are carved in this studio shop. There are usually some extraordinarily beautiful fireplace mantels and many other homemade items to purchase. Because this is real carving, every piece is one-of-a-kind.

I'm not a woodcarving aficionado, but apparently this shop is quite sought out as a place to explore carving tools and blocks. You can purchase any of the unique and intricate tools, along with books and patterns. The crafters will be happy to give advice and help you select tools.

HILLSIDE GENERAL STORE AND TASTE TRADERS

These two shops are adjacent to each other and just down the path from Valley Wood Carvers. Taste Traders carries lots of things sold in jars. Apple butter, hot sauces, jellies, jams, and syrups all carry the Dollywood logo. Again, these items make great gifts.

Next door, the Hillside General Store has less Dollywood merchandise and more traditional "five and dime" type stuff. There is a large porch with rocking chairs where you can sit and play checkers (both the chairs and checkers can be purchased inside). Colorful tin bakeware, wall hangings, dishes, and linens fill the shelves. The Hillside General Store also contains a post office that offers a special Dollywood postmark.

OLD FLAMES CANDLES

A tribute to Dolly's 1980 song, *Old Flames Can't Hold a Candle to You*, this popular shop makes thousands of candles everyday. You won't believe the variety of shapes, sizes, and colors. Of course, you just can't have a candle shop in Craftsman's Valley without the opportunity to dip your own. Pick a white candle and make it as colorful as you want.

My favorite candles in this shop are those that look, and smell, like various Southern delicacies. Different types of cobbler and bread-shaped candles come complete with little cast-iron skillets.

As an interesting note, the name of this shop has once again risen to the top. In August of 2017, Dolly recorded a version of *Old Flames Can't Hold a Candle to You* with R&B superstar Kesha. (The song was written by Kesha's mother and Dolly's longtime friend, Pebe Sebert.) The recording went all the way to number one on the *Billboard* pop chart.

VALLEY EXHIBITION HALL

Between Hillside General Store and Old Flames Candles, look up the hill and notice a barn that requires a short steep climb to enter. This is the Valley Exhibition Hall. Often, you won't have a reason to explore this space. However, periodically Dollywood will use this large barn for various exhibits or special presentations. During the 25th anniversary season in 2011, the Valley Exhibition Hall hosted a historical exhibit about Dollywood featuring artifacts and photographs.

During Smoky Mountain Christmas, Valley Exhibition Hall is transformed into the hyper-jingle world of Rudolph's Holly Jolly Junction. Based upon the famously nostalgic 1964 television special, this is the world of Rudolph the Red-Nosed Reindeer, his girlfriend Clarice, the misfit toys, and even the Abominable Snow Monster himself. Here is your chance to take the perfect Christmas card photo with the iconic characters that make millions of Americans smile each year. (Except, perhaps, the Snow Monster. I was terrified of him as a child—it didn't help that I was convinced he lived in our basement. I really don't want him on my Christmas card.) In addition to the photos, you can play a variety of reindeer games to win stuffed versions of the famous characters and decorate a cookie from Clarice's kitchen. To learn more about Dollywood's unique connection to Rudolph the Red-Nosed Reindeer, see "Dollywood History" at the end of chapter 1.

DAREDEVIL FALLS

Daredevil Falls is another great example of Dollywood's use of natural topography to elevate their rides. Tucked back into the trees on a hill overlooking the valley, this water ride easily blends into its mountain surroundings. Think of this ride as Dollywood's version of the traditional log-flume experience.

After you climb up the hill, you are loaded two by two into a huge log that holds up to eight people. Relax as you float through an abandoned logging camp and then scream as you plunge down the last drop. You will not get as wet on Daredevil Falls as you do on the Smoky Mountain River Rampage, but you will feel splashed from the ending plunge. There are lockers near the entrance for your valuables. Daredevil Falls is not open during Smoky Mountain Christmas.

COASTER FACTS: DAREDEVIL FALLS

Length: 1,350 feet
Tallest Drop: 67 feet
Max Speed: 50 mph
Duration: 3 minutes 56 seconds

VALLEY FORGE BLACKSMITH AND FOUNDRY

The large barn at the base of Daredevil Falls is the home of Dollywood's resident blacksmiths. These artisans amaze me as they effortlessly pound hot metal into graceful curves. The sights, sounds, and smells of the foundry are authentic and there is a nice covered platform to view all the action. This is the very blacksmith

I mentioned earlier when writing about the maintenance of Dollywood's vintage train engines.

These people can make anything: flower hooks, towel bars, signs for all occasions, ornaments, and tools. There is a very large selection of unique wind chimes. I'm amazed at the rich tones these large chimes create. If you live in a remote area, feel free to purchase a wind chime as a remembrance of your time at Dollywood. If you live next door to me...well, have you had a chance to see how beautiful the flower hooks are?

Anything you purchase here will last forever. Metal items might be cheaper back home, but the quality is far less. Several years ago, my parents gave my husband and me a sign from the Dollywood Blacksmith that says "Squirrel Crossing." The sign still looks brand new even though it has been through one Dollywood summer and numerous Minnesota winters.

HICKORY HOUSE BAR-B-Q

In 2009, *Amusement Business Magazine* named the pulled pork sandwich at Hickory House as the best single food item of any theme park in the United States. The sandwich smells as good as it tastes and is worthy of all the honors it acquires. Usually served with fries and beans, the meat is always placed on a fresh bun. The Hickory House also offers chicken strips on its limited quick-service menu.

Once again, cross back to the other side of the valley and enter a viewing area where you can see thin netting separate you from a steep hill. Take a deep breath because you are about to see one of the truly great sights of Dollywood.

EAGLE MOUNTAIN SANCTUARY

With 30,000 square feet, the area under the netting is the world's largest aviary for nonreleasable bald eagles. However, do not get the idea that this is a depressing place to look at sick birds. The wooded natural terrain is as dignified and majestic as the animals it protects. You will see the eagles; I've never been to Dollywood and not seen several of them in the trees. There are some permanent binoculars that you can pay to use if you want to get a closer look.

The bald eagles do not belong to Dollywood and are not cared for by park hosts. Dollywood graciously donates the land to the American Eagle Foundation who cares for the birds under permits from both the US Fish and Wildlife Service and the Tennessee Wildlife Resources Agency. The American Eagle Foundation also uses the sanctuary to rehabilitate releasable eagles. I love that part of my park admission is used to maintain this facility.

EAGLE'S NEST SHOP

Back in the valley, the closest shop to the sanctuary is, appropriately, the Eagle's Nest Shop. The American Eagle Foundation is a not-for-profit organization that relies on support from various sources, including Dollywood, to survive. All proceeds from the Eagle's Nest Shop are given to the American Eagle Foundation. In here, you can find practically anything you'd ever want with an image of an eagle on it.

Don't miss the large replica of an Eagle's nest between the shop and the sanctuary.

WINGS OF AMERICA THEATER

If you want to see these magnificent creatures in action, see the *Wings of America* show at the nearby theater. The outdoor theater is covered and features a film screen so you can watch the animals as they appear in the wild. There are always several birds of prey featured in the show including falcons, hawks, owls, and all sorts of things with wings. Of course, a bald eagle makes a prominent appearance.

The birds are well trained and cared for as they fly around the audience and land on strategic marks. The trainers, who work for the American Eagle Foundation, will ensure your safety by reminding you constantly to remove hats, food, and any trace of fur you may be wearing. This show is fascinating and perhaps the most educational opportunity in the park.

Outside and adjacent the theater are the homes of the birds featured in the show. Here, you can get a very close look at them. However, please note that the birds of prey rule the roost around here and the trainers will not tolerate any bad behavior from park guests. Likewise, the cast of the bird show can change depending upon who does or does not want to fly-in for work that day.

Wings of America is not presented during Smoky Mountain Christmas. If a summer baseball cap distracts the birds, I can't imagine how they'd handle Grandma's new fur earmuffs. Instead, the theater becomes home to *Chrismas Songbook*. Dolly's niece, Jada Star, joins her singing partner Barry J for a Christmas version of their popular show. This holiday offering is amazing and something I will never miss when I'm in the park. Their voices blend so beautifully that it's often hard to tell if they are humans or actual angels. It's also quite fitting that *Christmas Songbook* is performed inside the same theater as the bird presentation—both shows soar.

KAMAN'S ART SHOPPES

Believe it or not, we still have a bit of a journey yet to make in Craftsman's Valley, including two roller coasters. As you leave the vicinity of the bird theater, Kaman's Art Shoppes is the first location you will find. Here, artists are on staff to create either a funny caricature or realistic portrait of you and your group. There is also face painting available.

LUCKY 7 MINE & GEM SHOP

Across the path from Kaman's you can find hundreds, possibly thousands of geologic wonders filling the gem shop. Even if you have no intention of hauling rocks around the park, go inside to gawk at the variety of colors and sparkles found in nature. Small stones contained in barrels to huge crystals weighing several pounds can be found here.

The hosts at the Lucky 7 Gem Shop are well educated on their product and will happily answer questions. Unless you're on some kind of extreme workout program, this is one store where you'll for sure want to use package pick-up.

CALICO FALLS SCHOOLHOUSE

As you make your way up the path from Lucky 7 to the schoolhouse, a service-animal relief area is on your left; it is connected to the schoolhouse and clearly marked. If you have a service dog with you in the park, remember this location as it's the only one inside Dollywood. There is a second service-animal relief area right outside the front gate near Doggywood.

Calico Falls Schoolhouse is permanently stuck in 1890 so that modern kids, and all of us, can see how much has changed over the last 120 years. Slate boards sit on the desks in place of iPads and you won't find a cafeteria or gymnasium. What you will find are the chairs where excited, and probably sometimes mischievous, students sat to learn about the world around them. You can also spot the teacher's desk and supplies. If you visit during Smoky Mountain Christmas, you can see the holiday decorations that the students are making on their desks.

BLAZING FURY

One of the older rides at Dollywood, go on this indoor coaster for kitschy fun. Do not go on this ride expecting to be amazed by the animatronics or thrilled by any intense drops. Very tame and suitable for all ages, Blazing Fury is one of the only rides old enough to have a base of nostalgic fans. This means that the ride will stick around, but also ensures that any changes are met with harsh criticism.

After boarding the train you slowly roll past a series of vignettes showing an Old West town on fire. Firefighters and their old-fashioned pump wagons are around, as are plenty of saloon girls in distress. As you pass through the fire, keep your eyes open for a signpost giving directions to other imaginary towns. Notice that the sign is actually paying homage to all the former names of the park.

There are really only three small drops at the end of the ride. The drops themselves are nothing major, but they occur in the dark and could be startling for some riders. Blazing Fury is completely enclosed and makes a nice escape from the sun or rain.

COASTER FACTS: BLAZING FURY

Length: 1,500 feet
Tallest Drop: 20 feet
Max Speed: 25 mph
Duration: 3 minutes 20 seconds

GAMES AND ARCADE

As you exit Blazing Fury and head toward the end of the valley, you will see a large collection of games. While the games in Country Fair tend to draw a preteen crowd, the games here are full of teenagers. Also like the fair, the games and prizes change frequently, so you'll have to experience the current versions without my explanation. The games of Craftsman's Valley start near Blazing Fury and extend all the way around the bend and into Wilderness Pass.

TENNESSEE TORNADO

Ever feel like you want to hurl yourself through a mountain? Yep, a lot of us have those moments during our normal workday. Well here at Dollywood, you can take advantage of the ingenious use of topography and fly right through a foothill. Another great use of the natural surroundings, Tennessee Tornado loops its way over, around, and through the hills and trees.

This is a major steel coaster with several inversions and a 137-foot drop. One of the inversions is a full 360-degree circle. The coaster is well themed as an old mining train that got hit by a tornado.

While on the Tennessee Tornado you will have your picture taken on one of the drops. You can view and purchase your photo at the end of the ride. Also, due to the inversions, be careful of any loose items you have with you. There are lockers by the entrance if you need to use them.

COASTER FACTS: TENNESSEE TORNADO

Length:	2,682 feet
Tallest Drop:	137 feet
Max Speed:	70 mph
Duration:	1 minute 48 seconds

Now, turn back toward the valley and consider the journey you have made. Not only have you walked a considerable distance, but you've taken a symbolic pilgrimage through history from the grist mill to a steel roller coaster. You've hopefully learned a bit about how things were made in days past and you've marveled at the majesty of the bald eagle. Craftsman's Valley is unique to Dollywood and is quite a tribute to where we've been and where we are heading.

WILDERNESS PASS

It's fitting that Wilderness Pass is tucked the farthest into the hills, as it most closely resembles the national park. It's also fitting that it's a "pass" because it connects the two long parallel sides of the park. Wilderness Pass is the youngest land with the newest rides and nicest restrooms. While the other lands of Dollywood celebrate the people's way of living in the mountains, Wilderness Pass celebrates nature itself and our desire to protect it.

As you curve through this land and the neighboring Timber Canyon, it will become clear that these lands were designed with the future in mind. There is a noticeable lack of shops and buffets. Instead, these lands hold the cutting-edge thrill rides and quick-service eateries that appeal to a new generation. Parents and Grandparents may hold the purse strings, but if the teens aren't happy...ain't nobody happy. Dollywood realizes that if families are to continue to visit, the park must remain attractive to the youth.

GAMES/ARCADE

Wilderness Pass begins with more games geared toward the teenage crowd. Parents may see this as a place to spend money trying to win a prize that would have cost half the amount if they had just bought it at a store. But I agree with the teens, the amount of effort spent attempting to win is worth the extra money. A stuffed animal from the store is just that. A stuffed animal won in a game comes already attached with memories and a story.

WILD EAGLE

Find the enormous steel eagle—you can't miss it—and enter the path that takes you toward the beautiful blue rails that rise into the sky. Here is the entrance to Wild Eagle, the first winged roller coaster in the United States. This is a major ride and one of the crown jewels of Dollywood's impressive coaster collection.

A winged coaster is one where the riders hang over the sides of the track. There is no train that sits on top of the rails. With this design, riders feel like they are flying because there is nothing above or below them.

Notice how, once again, Dollywood uses the natural topography. The first hill of the coaster extends from the top of a real hill to reach its apex of twenty-one stories. Wild Eagle is the only Dollywood ride that is visible from the parking lots. Because the ride includes inversions, you must be able to fit into the safety harness in order to ride. There are test seats located by the entrance so you can try the harness without waiting in line. Use the lockers, also by the entrance, for your loose items as you will definitely turn upside-down on the Wild Eagle.

For me, the best part of this coaster is the amazing theming of the ride itself. The ride system, on which the riders hang, is concealed beneath huge bald eagles. When the ride makes the first drop and dips into the first inversion, the eagles gracefully follow the curve as if in synchronized flight. Since its debut in 2012, other theme parks have added winged coasters, but none are as themed as Wild Eagle.

COASTER FACTS: WILD EAGLE

Length: 3,127 feet
Tallest Drop: 135 feet
Max Speed: 61 mph
Duration: 2 minutes 22 seconds

EAGLE'S FLIGHT OUTFITTER'S

As you exit the Wild Eagle, a small shop sells many items with the coaster's logo. It's easy to brag that you were able to brave the ride if you purchase the "I'm an eagle!" T-shirt. (The shop also sells a "I'm a chicken!" T-shirt for those that weren't quite able to make it on the ride.) You can buy Wild Eagle postcards in case you want to let the folks back home know of your courageous journey.

Butterfly Wisdom

Before you leave the Wild Eagle area, take some time to contemplate the enormous steel eagle. This is not just an ornament for the ride entrance, it's actually a world-famous sculpture. Commissioned by Dollywood for this very location, the sculpture was designed and crafted by Canadian artist Kevin Stone. Stone is known worldwide for his work with steel and the ability to create intricate details on large rigid surfaces. On this sculpture, he welded thousands of steel feathers that he made individually.

The eagle's wingspan is forty-eight feet and it stands two stories high. The enormous talons are open and it's obvious this eagle is in the final stages of swooping for prey. Needless to say, this sculpture makes a fantastic photograph.

SKYVIEW SNACKS

This small snack bar is mainly for beverages. It's a great place to refill the Dollywood mug because it offers the largest variety of sodas and frozen drinks. There is also popcorn available here.

FIREHOUSE FUN YARD

We haven't seen a children's play area since way back in Owens Farm. This charming yard is well-themed with several activities for kids.

Firehouse Fun Yard offers both wet and dry play spaces. A structure themed as a fire engine is a dry place where children can climb and try out all the gadgets. Nearby, there is a splash zone for use when the weather is hot and humid. The splash zone does not operate when it's cold outside.

Please know that this area of the park gets quite warm in the heat of the summer. There aren't as many trees back here and the sun can get intense. Dollywood has installed several shades that stretch over the walking paths and there are a few misting machines in Wilderness Pass. Just remember that you can always get free water at SkyView Snacks.

FIRECHASER EXPRESS

Fires in the Great Smoky Mountain National Park are carefully observed and controlled to preserve the natural beauty. FireChaser Express is Dollywood's tribute to the men and women who manage dangerous fires. This area of the park is also a tribute to the people who worked tirelessly during the rare 2016 fire that did get out of control.

Opened in 2014, FireChaser Express was the first dual-launch family roller coaster in the nation. A launch coaster is one that does not rely on a chain to pull the train up the first hill. Instead, powerful magnets and electric current are used to quickly propel the train with enough force to clear the first drop. A family coaster is a new trend of ride that many theme parks are scrambling to design. These coasters are more intense than the typical kiddie-coaster, but they are not anywhere as extreme as most other roller coasters. FireChaser Express is the first coaster designed for families that features two launches.

After boarding the train, you are launched forward through a series of curves. There is one area where a chain lifts you a bit higher, then more drops and curves follow. There are no inversions and you are never upside down on this attraction. At some point, the train becomes stuck in Crazy Charlie's Gas and Fireworks Emporium. Why does the national park allow Crazy Charlie to have this flammable store in the forest? We don't know and he's not around to ask. But suddenly, the largest firework explodes and the train is launched backward through another series of curves.

This ride is smooth, quick, and a lot of fun. The theming of both the station and ride is exceptional. Now, let me introduce the big family coaster debate. It seems that it's difficult to design a coaster intense enough to appeal to the teenagers, but mild enough to attract small kids and grandparents. So, most of the family coasters lean one way or the other. I think FireChaser Express leans a bit to the teenager side. The tallest drop is not exactly small and the backward launch can be disconcerting. If in doubt, have a few from your group ride and let them decide if the rest can handle it.

COASTER FACTS: FIRECHASER EXPRESS

Length:	2,426 feet
Tallest Drop:	79 feet
Max Speed:	34.5 mph
Duration:	2 minutes 19 seconds

SPLINTER'S SNACKS AND DOGHOUSE

Splinter is a crafty squirrel that wanted some of your theme park budget. He jumped at the opportunity and constructed two quick-service eateries that are just so darn cute. Look above the building and notice the village where Splinter and all his squirrel friends live. Since their decorating involves mostly the use of acorns, it's good for us that they serve people food down below.

At Trailside Snacks, you can find all sorts of sweet things made with ice cream and/or cake batter. Vanilla soft-serve is mixed with peaches, strawberries, or cookies to make a creamy dessert. Floats and chocolate soft-serve is also available. Splinter's offers the most diverse collection of funnel cakes at the park. You can try a plain funnel cake, or one with hot fudge, strawberries, cinnamon sugar, and ice cream.

Next door at the Doghouse, enjoy a large selection of hotdogs served on freshly made buns. All the usual toppings and beverages are available.

VOLUNTEER SUPPLY COMPANY

This is a great shop for those summer necessities that tend to break or disappear in theme parks. Sunglasses, flip-flops, and water shoes are sold here. Also, this is the one shop at Dollywood that carries merchandise themed to FireChaser Express.

THE PLAZA AT WILDERNESS PASS

Opened in 2018, The Plaza at Wilderness Pass is not only new to Dollywood but is also unique among all theme parks. Disney offers a similar experience aboard its cruise ships, however, here at Dollywood this immersive and entertaining attraction is included without any additional expense.

You'll know you're in the right place when you walk through several arches covered with foliage that reflects the park's current season. Traditionally at Dollywood, thrill rides were placed in this part of the park and entertainment offerings were located toward the front entrance. But it's clear that this approach has changed in recent years. Lightning Rod's placement in Jukebox Junction and The Plaza location here in Wilderness Pass signals a desire for the park to redirect traffic. Now, thrill seekers have a reason to visit Dollywood's front half and others have a purpose to venture toward the back.

A large fountain occupies the center of The Plaza at Wilderness Pass. This fountain is themed to reflect the streams found inside Great Smoky Mountains National Park. It's simply stunning. Around the fountain are large areas to relax. You'll notice a structure toward the back of the plaza that looks like the porch to a large national park lodge. Feel free to grab a rocking chair or to sit on the grass and enjoy whatever is happening on the day of your visit.

The Plaza at Wilderness Pass hosts interactive experiences that are themed to the park's current season. You never know what you will find and you can discover the day's lineup in the daily showtimes guide. Basically, this is the place for smaller, more informal types of concerts. You won't sit in a theater here—and that's what makes this venue such a unique space. You'll get to sit and relax right near the performers who may even ask you to clap or drum along. You will find storytellers, singers, dulcimer players, drummers—virtually an endless variety of performing artists at The Plaza. And, don't worry if you are not in the mood to participate as there are lots of spots to sit and just enjoy.

Dollywood's Smoky Mountain Christmas comes to The Plaza in a big way. A ginormous high-tech tree fills the space over the fountain. This tree is capable of displaying multitudes of colors and other special effects. You'll also discover that the performing artists are in the holiday mood as their demonstrations/performances take on a decidedly Christmas flavor.

Linger as long as you want in The Plaza. When you are ready, continue toward to the large creepy abandoned mine that looms ahead.

The plaza signals that we have come to an end of Wilderness Pass. As you curve around and head toward the large mine looming up ahead, notice a cute sculpture of two owls hatching out of their eggs. This is a great spot to take a photo. The owls even have "Dollywood" painted on their nest so you can remember where you were when the photo was taken.

Wilderness Pass gave us plenty of opportunities to enjoy ourselves in the mountains. Hopefully, this very small taste of the national park will give you a desire to visit the real thing before your Smoky Mountain vacation is complete. But for now, it's time to visit the newest of Dollywood's lands. Walk toward the scary mine, but take a sharp right as you cross under the old mine tracks. Continue up the incline and through the hollow trunk of an enormous tree.

WILDWOOD GROVE

Opened in 2019, Wildwood Grove is Dollywood's version of Fantasyland. The largest single expansion in the park's history, Wildwood Grove opened complete with restaurants, rides, shops, and the spectacular Wildwood Tree.

The park created a bit of a story about the background of Wildwood Grove. Apparently, a young girl wondered away from the lumber camp of nearby Timber Canyon. After following a butterfly, she ended up exploring an unknown part of the Smoky Mountain wilderness. A group of loggers set out to search for her. When they found the young girl, she was laughing under an enormous tree that glowed with butterflies. (The story ends there. I'd like to alert you that it may not be the best idea for you, especially if you're a child, to wander after a butterfly into an unknown forest. This type of activity is best left to the minds of theme park designers and Dolly Parton.)

You'll know you're on the doorstep of Wildwood Grove when you see an amazing fountain off to your right. If you look closely, you'll notice that the falling streams of water are actually the strings of a giant harp. You can hear the harp playing in the breeze. The combination of sculpture and fountain is the perfect way to introduce visitors to this wonderful world of whimsy and fantasy.

TILL & HARVEST 🍽

It may seem odd to find a Mexican restaurant in the middle of the Smoky Mountains, but in this land of fantasy anything can happen—and at this eatery it happens well. Even though this place is still new, I'm predicting that the Smoky Mountain Nachos at Till & Harvest will become a permanent fixture at Dollywood. A large layer of tortilla chips are covered with Dollywood's own freshly made pulled pork. Then, you can choose which of the many toppings to finish off the dish, including: cheese, vegetables, guacamole, and salsas.

If the Smoky Mountain Nachos are too many calories for you, Till & Harvest offers the best healthy option in the entire park. The Sizzling Steak Salad is a fresh salad with your choice of ingredients that is topped with marinated steak strips. Everything at Till & Harvest can be customized right in front of you—and everything is fresh.

After getting food inside the large restaurant, diners can eat at Till & Harvest's large covered patio. This is a great place to eat and enjoy the harp fountain.

SWEETS AND TREATS

Attached to the outside of Till & Harvest is this quick-service snack shop that offers the usual park fare. Again, you can eat your food at the covered patio.

TREETOP TOWER

Remember Splinter...the squirrel that runs a snack shop over in Wilderness Pass? Well, Treetop Tower is his dream ride. Here, the entire family can sit inside giant acorns that rise and rotate. It's a quite tame ride and even those with motion sickness should be okay. And while the tower doesn't go that high, the views are surprisingly great.

GREAT TREE SWING

This is Dollywood's version of the ubiquitous pirate ship ride that is found is many parks across the world. Except, Wildwood Grove's version takes its inspiration from nature and looks like a giant tree swing.

WILDWOOD CREEK

Because it's the newest land in Dollywood, the vegetation isn't as lush yet. Consequently, it can get quite hot and humid back here—especially during the summer months. Wildwood Creek is a water feature that allows guests to splash in a beautiful creek. In fact, the creek flows down a small hill and under a lovely bridge, creating more perfect photo places.

You can get as wet as you (or the kid next to you) wants to be. Be advised: if there are any number of kids in the water, you are sure to get splashed at least a little. When you are finished cooling off, cross the creek and keep on the lookout for some vicious wild animals up ahead.

BLACK BEAR TRAIL

This ride is simply awesome—I haven't seen anything like it at any other park. Black Bear Trail is one of those rides that as much fun to watch as it is to experience. Here, guests ride adorable fiberglass bears as they journey through a landscaped trail of Smoky Mountain colors. Don't let the seemingly childish aspect of the attraction impact you—this ride is for the entire family and you are sure to see many adults riding their own bear. Needless to say, the photo opportunities while watching this ride are endless.

MOUNTAIN GROVE MERCHANTS

Mountain Grove Merchants is the only shop inside Wildwood Grove. It's not overly large and sells items specific to this area of the park: think butterflies, dragonflies, frogs, bears, and leaves. Most of the merchandise in this shop is not available anywhere else at Dollywood. This thing I love best about this shop is that park designers included the intricate trunk of a real tree in its design.

FROGS & FIREFLIES

Wildwood Grove truly has something for everyone. Frogs & Fireflies is for the kids that still get a kick of riding in an animal around a circle. The animal this time is a frog and they revolve as they chase fireflies.

As you depart Frogs & Fireflies and walk toward the enormous tree up ahead, look to your right and notice a small covered pavilion. This is where the characters of Wildwood Grove pose for pictures and chat with guests. You never know who may be welcoming guests at this place, but they are as charming and whimsical as the land itself. Check *This Week at Dollywood* on the day of your adventure to discover the times for character meetings.

THE WILDWOOD TREE

The Wildwood Tree is the focus of Wildwood Grove, and rightfully so—it is spectacular. Even though it looks like it's always been there, the Wildwood Tree is Dolly-made. It rises 52 feet in the air and includes 9,000 individually fabricated leaves. But you must get closer to see the true beauty of this monument. Among the leaves are 300 fantastic butterflies that glow day and night. And don't miss the subtle carvings in the tree's trunk as you will discover musical instruments that are important in Smoky Mountain life.

The Wildwood Tree is similar in scope to the Tree of Life at Disney's Animal Kingdom down in Orlando. It is sure to become as much a symbol of Dollywood as the grist mill and the Dollywood Express.

At night the tree comes to life—almost literally. Every fifteen minutes, the lights in Wildwood Grove dim and you will suddenly hear Dolly's captivating voice. She will tell a story as the tree "reacts" to her words. Using lights and sound, the tree can simulate everything from a spring day to a frightening Smoky Mountain thunderstorm. The butterflies at night are especially amazing as they change through an unlimited array of colors. The Wildwood Tree is a technological marvel.

During Smoky Mountain Christmas the Wildwood Tree's evening show glows with the colors of the season. The butterflies are, of course, red and green while Dolly sings one of my favorite holiday songs: *I'll Be Home with Bells On*. Dolly also tells a bit of a story and you should watch the tree carefully for an amazing effect when she mentions the Christmas star.

HIDDEN HOLLOW

If it's extremely humid out, you may find that Hidden Hollow might be your most favorite attraction in all of Wildwood Grove. Hidden Hollow, directly across from the tree, is a large indoor play area that is completely air-conditioned. It's rather dark in here—which may or may not be a good thing depending upon your perspective.

There are places to sit on both benches and the large floor. But any kid in your party is sure to have their own party on the gigantic play structure that wraps around the room. A lot of extra energy can be burned off here. Also note: Hidden Hollow is heated in the winter if you need a place to warm-up during Smoky Mountain Christmas.

THE MAD MOCKINGBIRD

Everything that's old is new again. This type of amusement ride was popular in the 1970's and then fell out of fashion as new technology took over. However, for some unknown reason, parks across the world have re-discovered the attraction and they are popping up everywhere.

Each mockingbird is a swing that rotates around a center column. As they rotate, good old-fashioned centrifugal force causes them to float on air—there is no hydraulic technology here.

DRAGONFLIER

Dragonflier is Dollywood's newest coaster. I love it! It's as smooth and quiet as...well...a dragonfly.

Dragonflier is a family coaster and is often compared to Fire-Chaser Express over in Wilderness Pass. I find that it's about the same in intensity. Dragonflier is a suspended coaster, meaning that the riders are hanging from the track on seats that are able to swing with the movement of the ride. You will not want to keep your flip-flops on your feet while riding Dragonflier—Dollywood provides storage bins for use during the ride.

What I love about Dragonflier is how it stays low to the ground. During one section, the coaster gracefully flies underground through a series of curves. I enjoy the feeling of flying over the landscaped beautify of Wildwood Grove without the worry of losing my stomach.

Because of its popularity, the lines can be a bit long. Check the Dollywood app to see what they are like before you venture into Wilderness Grove. This may be a good use of your TimeSaver, if you've purchased one, but remember that Dragonflier can only be ridden once using this method.

COASTER FACTS: DRAGONFLIER

Length:	1,486 feet
Tallest Drop:	63 feet
Max Speed:	46 mph
Duration:	1 minute exactly

The graceful Dragonflier signals that your visit to Wildwood Grove has come to an end. Due to the difference in elevation, there is no way to continue to the rest of the park except by back-tracking the way you came. So take another stroll through Wildwood Grove. Gaze at the amazing Wildwood Tree and take a last gander at the delightful bears of Black Bear Trail. Walk past Till & Harvest and cross again through the hollow tree trunk. When you get down the incline and see the terrifying mine, take a right.

TIMBER CANYON

You'll know you've left Wildwood Grove when the whimsical butterflies are gone and a creepy animatronic buzzard squawks at you. You're now in Timber Canyon, a former center of mining and logging that was abandoned for some unknown reason. Hovering high above you is the giant tin remnant of an old mine. Even on a sunny day, the mine looks menacing and the screams coming from within do little to calm your nerves. Notice how the music has changed to help you transition to this new land.

Timber Canyon is the most exposed land in the park and always seems to be ten degrees warmer than anywhere else. Dollywood has taken some action on this account by installing water-misters and providing more canopies over seating areas. During summer, it's important to stay hydrated in the canyon, especially if you're a teen jumping from coaster to coaster all day.

MYSTERY MINE

The large building I referred to earlier is the home of Mystery Mine and the first structure you will notice in Timber Canyon. In my opinion, Mystery Mine is the most intense ride at Dollywood, although others may argue with me.

Mystery Mine is a highly themed steel roller coaster that runs through an abandoned coal mine. There are creepy surprises everywhere in both the queue and ride that makes Mystery Mine the closest thing Dollywood has to a haunted house. You can see some of the Mystery Mine's outdoor track as it twists and turns above the path. However, please note, most of this ride occurs inside the structure. You can't see the completely vertical drop, but believe me, it's in there!

This coaster does an excellent job of combining special effects into the ride itself. You won't be able to miss the use of fire and steam. Your photo will be taken during one of the drops so that you can see what you looked like in the darkness. Mystery Mine is an especially fun ride to watch as a spectator. Sitting in the shadow of the ride in one of the few shady spots around Timber Canyon is a nice way to watch your loved ones come racing (and screaming) out of the building.

This is another coaster that has numerous inversions. You must be able to fully fit within the safety restraint; there is a test seat near the ride's entrance. Lockers are located across the path from the entrance for all your loose items.

COASTER FACTS: MYSTERY MINE

Length:	1,811 feet
Tallest Drop:	85 feet
Max Speed:	46 mph
Duration:	2 minutes 30 seconds

THE MINE SHAFT

If you haven't had enough of Mystery Mine and want to take a piece of it home with you, purchase a souvenir in this shop. This is a bigger shop than it looks as you pass by and you can find other items of attire and jewelry. There are usually some colorful tie-dye Dollywood shirts sold here.

Butterfly Wisdom

Ten Dolly Inspired Attractions Dollywood Needs to Add

1. I Will Always Tunnel of Love You
   Float in the darkness with your sweetheart and listen to Whitney Houston's version of "I Will Always Love You." When the dramatic pause and loud downbeat happens, plunge down three hundred feet as you realize the song is about breaking up with someone.

MICHAEL FRIDGEN

2. Spinners of Many Colors
   Sit inside this tilt-a-whirl inspired ride with cars painted a multitude of colors. As you spin, animatronic kids point and laugh at you.

3. Steel Magnolias Hair Salon
   Have your hair cut and styled like a football helmet while eating an armadillo-shaped cake.

4. Dolly's Wig Emporium
   Located next door to Steel Magnolias Hair Salon, visit this shop if your haircut doesn't work for you.

5. Islands in the Stream River Rafts
   Ride on a sailboat through the most raging rapids in the Smokies. But, watch out for the islands—if you hit one, a 1983 synthesizer blasts in your ear.

6. Dolly's 70s Swings
   Ride on swings modeled after the one Dolly used in her 1976 television variety series. While the swings move in a large circle, an animatronic Barbara Mandrell throws pies at you.

7. Closer to Heaven Shoe Shoppe
   Every pair of shoes in this store has a six-inch heel...even the bedroom slippers!

8. Dolly's Time Travel Adventure
   On this 4-D experience, let Dolly's physicians turn back the clock. You will emerge looking years younger. A Dollywood Season Pass is required because there is a four-to-six-week recovery period.

9. The Chicken Ranch Restaurant
   An adults-only establishment. Extra charges apply.

10. Nine-to-Five: The Game
    You get three chances to hit a photo of your boss with a water-balloon. If you make a direct hit, you win a box of artificial sweetener.

LUMBERJACK LIFTS

Frankly, I find this ride to be a bit bizarre because it requires work—and who wants to work while on vacation? On Lumberjack Lifts, you sit with a partner and pull on a rope to levitate your seats. Yes, you have to provide the power required to run the ride. The tower is twenty-five feet high and there is actually a pretty good view from the top. Don't worry if you drop the rope. The ride has a mechanism to ensure that seats descend slowly and safely.

You'll see a lot of parent/child combos on this ride—try to smile and let the kid think they are doing most of the work. Also, go on this ride before the buffet, not after.

LUMBER JACK'S PIZZA

Remember when I said that it's hard to get a deal on Dollywood tickets? Well, at Lumber Jack's you can actually get a free Super Gold Pass—keep reading.

Of course, Lumber Jack's Pizza serves pizza of all varieties. You can purchase by the slice, whole pizzas, and even an extra-large thirty-inch pie that can feed ten people. This restaurant also offers strombolis, salads, bread sticks, and Italian subs.

There are many tables on the side of Lumber Jack's that have canopies for shade, but I like the umbrella tables located directly across the path. These tables are surrounded by water. Formally a site for a ride since removed, the water creates a nice atmosphere.

All right, so you still want those free Dollywood Super Gold Passes? Take the Lumber Jack's pizza challenge. You and a buddy will be served a twelve-pound, thirty-inch pizza that is loaded with bacon, ham, sausage, pepperoni, chicken, and vegetables. Of course, the pizza is also covered with pounds of cheese. If you and your partner can finish the entire pizza in one hour, you will each win a Dollywood Super Gold Pass. The cost of the challenge is $75, but two super gold passes would usually be $214 each. I have no information on how many people have completed or failed the challenge. Do not ride on the Dizzy Disc for at least two weeks after eating this much food.

DROP LINE

Once upon a time, a drop line was a real thing. Before the national park, when logging was permitted in the Smoky Mountains, the early loggers lacked large diesel vehicles that could transport timber down the sides of mountains. At the time, loggers stretched a long cable between the peaks of two adjacent mountains. There was a metal catch in the middle of this cable that included a secondary cable which dropped down to the valley below—this secondary cable was the drop line. When a tree on top of the mountain was ready, it was sent flying down the cable that stretched between the peaks. The soaring tree eventually hit the metal catch and was released from the main line. Then, the tree simply fell along the drop line until it landed on the ground. If this all sounds confusing, don't worry. There is a diagram of a drop line at Dollywood, right across the path from the attraction.

Drop Line is a 230-foot drop tower. Twenty-four guests are seated in a complete circle around a large metal tower. The circle is rotated and raised to the summit of the tower. At the top, guests are treated to extraordinary views of the Smoky Mountains as Drop Line rotates a few more times. Then, without little warning, the rotating stops and guests are sent plummeting to the ground at seventy-eight miles per hour.

For me, Drop Line is not as much intense as it is exhilarating. It's not the tallest drop tower on the planet—by any means—but it may offer the best views. However, please do not take out your phone and attempt to photograph the gorgeous view from the top, no matter how tempted you may be. When Dollywood hosts see that you have a phone or camera, they are required to stop the ride. Your Drop Line circle will slowly lower back to the loading platform and you will be asked to leave the ride. This happens more than you might expect and it's really annoying for everyone else waiting in line.

WHISTLE PUNK CHASER

Here is the kiddie coaster that you may have missed back in Country Fair. You can't miss Whistle Punk Chaser's bright orange track and ultra-cute train cars. This small coaster was new in 2017 and offers a smooth ride for the younger crowd. Between Whistle Punk Chaser, Lumberjack Lifts, and the Firehouse Fun Yard, there are plenty of things for little siblings to do while the others ride on the large coasters in this part of Dollywood.

THUNDERHEAD

Designing a new ride for a theme park is a bit like designing a new bathroom for your house. You can gather all the ideas, get them on paper, try some samples, and even use computer models, but you never really know how it's going to turn out. Every year, some parks win with a design and some lose. Thunderhead was a major win for Dollywood.

Everything came together better than planned and the theme park industry noticed. Winner of countless awards, Thunderhead is a wooden coaster that once again uses Dollywood's natural topography. It almost looks as if these massive piles of wood have always been there. The coaster is fast. I can't stress that enough…it's very fast. Thunderhead features the first fly-through station in the country. This means that while you are in the station waiting to board, a full train of passengers comes flying through the station elevated above the loading track. Even though I know it's coming, it scares me every time.

You will be photographed on this ride and the pictures are available at the exit. There are no inversions, though you still want to keep your loose articles secure. Thunderhead has that sound unique to wooden coasters and it's a thrill just to walk past.

COASTER FACTS: THUNDERHEAD

Length:	3,230 feet
Tallest Drop:	100 feet
Max Speed:	55 mph
Duration:	2 minutes 30 seconds

You'll still hear the rumbling thunder of the coaster as you take the winding path on your descent out of Timber Canyon. Your exit out of this land will be just as creepy as your entrance when you notice the graveyard and coffin. There are several excellent photo opportunities on the curved path that passes under the Dollywood Express railroad bridge. Don't miss the weird showers and pause for another photo. When you near the end of the path, you will see a familiar sight—Victorian shops of Showstreet and the gold Dollywood sign tell you that you've come full circle!

Immediately as you enter Showstreet, the special Dollywood exit to parking lots G and H is on your right. This is also the exit to catch the trolley back to Dollywood's DreamMore Resort.

Further up on your right is the Dollywood Emporium. Do some final shopping, pick up your packages in the back and exit the park. The parking trams are ready and waiting to escort you back to your vehicle. While on the tram, relax and think about your day. Take a mental snapshot of the moment and be grateful that you were able to experience this unique, truly American, theme park.

Hopefully, after your long day, you still remember where your car is parked. If you need any assistance, contact a tram operator and they will be more than happy to find someone who can help. Again, as you depart that parking lot, you will meander around the base of a mountain toward the same area where you entered. As you follow the signs for the park exit and approach the parking booths, don't miss Dollywood's official goodbye on the right. It's just a simple sign from Dolly stating, "I will always love you."

All traffic is directed to take a left onto McCarter Hollow Road. Then, if you are headed for Sevierville or Dollywood's DreamMore Resort, get into the right lane. All other traffic, including those heading toward Pigeon Forge and Gatlinburg, should take the left lanes (See Map 2: Arriving at Dollywood, found in the back of this guide.) The directions are also clearly marked on overhead signs. Now, go back to your hotel and sleep. Tomorrow, we have a whole other park to explore in Dolly's world.

CHAPTER 4

DOLLYWOOD'S SPLASH COUNTRY

ARRIVAL AND PARKING

A relaxing time in the sun is exactly what you need after an active day at Dollywood. So, take the same route that we used to get to Dollywood, turning off Veterans Boulevard and onto McCarter Hollow Road. (See Map 2: Arriving at Dollywood, found in the back of this guide.) Stop at the parking booths to take care of business and continue on your way. However, this time you will turn right and follow the sign for Dollywood's Splash Country. Drive underneath McCarter Hollow Road and enter the parking lot. (See Map 3: Dollywood Parking Lots, found in the back of this guide.)

This parking lot is considerably smaller than the one across the street. You will not need to use a tram to access Dollywood's Splash Country. Make sure you have everything you need, including towels and sunscreen, and walk to the entrance directly in front of you.

Remember this crucial information: you must have a separate Dollywood's Splash Country admission ticket to enter the park. Regular Dollywood passes and tickets will not work here.

Butterfly Wisdom

There is one universal law for all water parks on the planet: no matter where you are or what the weather is, if you want a lounge chair, get there early! Check dollywood.com for the opening time on the day you are visiting and arrive in the parking lot at least twenty minutes before. There are several areas of lounge chairs in the park and you should have a place in mind before opening. When you are allowed inside, proceed immediately to get settled on a lounge chair. You'll need your towels to show others that they are claimed.

People with younger children tend to congregate around Little Creek Falls or The Cascades. Older teens and adults usually prefer the areas of chairs around the wave pool, Mountain Waves. Make sure all those in your party know where your home base is for the day. Regular theme parks have all their guest services in the front of the park because guests tend to avoid a home base and move often. However, at most water parks, guests choose a centralized location as a home and come back to this place often. This is why the guest services at Dollywood's Splash Country are scattered throughout.

Once inside and settled, take a few moments to look around at the beauty of Dollywood's Splash Country. The park is lush with trees and hills; it is easily the best landscaped water park in the country. Notice how the major slides use the mountain to provide elevation. Observe the lazy river as it looks like it could be a natural mountain stream. This park is lovely and you have the whole day to enjoy.

SPECIAL RULES AND CONSIDERATIONS

Due to the inherent danger of water, all water parks have well-enforced rules and Dollywood's Splash Country is no exception. You must take a few minutes to familiarize yourself with park policies and to make sure any children understand how to stay safe. Remember, lifeguards are around to enforce rules and to respond to emergencies, but they are not responsible for the general safety of any guest.

- Kids under thirteen must be accompanied by someone older than sixteen at all times.
- Nonswimmers are required to wear lifejackets that can be found at Downbound Float Trip, Mountain Waves, Little Creek Falls, and The Cascades.
- You must obey all lifeguard instructions immediately, or you will be asked to leave the park without a refund.
- No footwear is allowed on the slides; however, swim shoes may be worn in the nonslide areas. Footwear with any sort of buckle is prohibited on all attractions.
- Glasses and sunglasses may be worn on all attractions, but they must have a head strap. Straps can be purchased at the Riverside Trading Post.
- Children who are not toilet trained must wear swim diapers.
- Do not swim if you aren't feeling well and/or if you have diarrhea.
- Wash your hands frequently with soap and water, especially after bathroom breaks and before eating.
- Frequently take your children on bathroom breaks.
- Always change your child's diaper in a bathroom and never in the park.
- Always wash thoroughly with soap and water before swimming.

Although it's not an official policy because Dollywood can't control what you do at your hotel, I feel strongly that everyone needs a good shower with soap and water after a day at a water park. You are probably very clean and diligent about health, but not all families in the water will share that same level of diligence. A nice shower not only cleans off any contaminates, but it also gets rid of any chlorine from your skin.

Water parks are fun places that can create a lot of memories. But at the same time, all water parks have guest safety as their number one priority. If you are reprimanded, please remember that the park employee is doing their job with your best interest and safety in mind.

SUNSCREEN

Do not argue with me about this. You must, must, must wear sunscreen all day long at Dollywood's Splash Country. Even on a cloudy day, the sun's ultraviolet radiation can cause severe burns in this part of the United States. Make sure your sunscreen is waterproof and reapply according to the manufacturer's directions. Sunscreen is available at all shops, and most food vendors, inside Dollywood's Splash Country.

First, wear sunscreen so you don't ruin the rest of your vacation. Sunburn is painful and causes dehydration and problems sleeping. You're spending a lot of time and money in the Smoky Mountains; make sure you enjoy every moment of it pain free. Parents, it's your responsibility to make sure that your children are covered at all times.

Second, wear sunscreen to prevent skin cancer. Please don't think I'm being reactionary and dramatic. I've seen the horrible result of too much sun. Skin cancer is disfiguring at best and deadly at worst. If there is someone in your party who is just too cool to wear sunscreen, Google "skin cancer pictures" and show them the result. According to the Mayo Clinic, people with darker skin tones, including African Americans, may not burn as easily, but they are just as susceptible to skin cancer as those with light skin. Everyone needs to wear sunscreen.

CENTRALIZED MEASURING

Centralized measuring is located at Splash and Dash Sundries in the middle of the park, near the entrance to the wave pool. Anyone around forty-eight inches in height should stop by the measuring station to get an official park measurement. After measuring, you will be given an armband that corresponds with the park map to let you know which attractions you can ride. As with most water parks, paper maps are not available at Dollywood's Splash Country because they are a nuisance when wet. Instead, large signs with permanent maps are posted throughout the park.

BATHHOUSES

While restrooms are scattered throughout, there are two bathhouses inside Dollywood's Splash Country. Each bathhouse offers private changing areas and showers. Make sure to shower thoroughly with soap and water before you visit a water attraction. The front bathhouse is located near the park entrance in the first large green building you will see. The second bathhouse is found near the bridge that crosses the lazy river by the wave pool.

GUESTS WITH DISABILITIES

As a general rule, water parks are never as accessible to those with disabilities as standard theme parks are. Rushing water, slick surfaces, and required stairs make for a less than fun experience if you have any mobility issues. Still, there are a number of attractions at Dollywood's Splash Country that are accessible. I've noted the rides that require stairs in this guide. The official park map also indicates the attractions that can be accessed easily. There are a number of restrooms for those with disabilities and all food vendors can accommodate everyone.

TIMESAVER

Dollywood's Splash Country has a line-jumping system also called TimeSaver H2O. Similar to Dollywood's version, TimeSaver reserves your place in line while you enjoy other attractions. However, instead of using a lanyard card, here users are issued a wristband and must visit kiosks around the park to select their next attraction. There are five kiosks and they are marked with a clock on park maps. The wristband alerts the rider when they can proceed to the attraction.

TimeSaver H2O at Dollywood's Splash Country costs $22.78 on top of regular park admission. For this option, the kiosk saves your place in line and informs you how long it will be before you can go on the ride. You may only use this regular version of TimeSaver H2O once for each attraction. But, for $31.89 you can purchase a Premium TimeSaver H2O that allows you to ride with only 50 percent the wait time. Again, you can use Premium TimeSaver H2O only once per attraction. Unlimited TimeSaver H2O costs $54.66 and allows guests to ride an unlimited number of attractions with a 50 percent wait time.

There is a $5 refundable deposit required and gold pass holders receive a $5 discount. Guests at Dollywood's DreamMore Resort do not receive a TimeSaver H2O, only the regular TimeSaver at the theme park across the parking lot.

Again, just as we did at Dollywood, we have to consider the worth of TimeSaver. It all depends upon how much you love water slides. I have a great time at Dollywood's Splash Country by lounging around and floating in the lazy river. I also enjoy the wave pool. TimeSaver H2O does not work for any of the things that I like to do. However, my niece and nephews absolutely love hurling themselves down the wet side of a mountain. If it's an especially busy day, $23 is a good investment for them because they get to ride more frequently. The most popular attraction at the park is RiverRush and I have seen the wait be as high as 2 hours! (Fortunately, it will likely be a lot less if you visit during the week and ride early or late.)

SUNNY MUNNY

Nobody wants to take their purse or wallet on a water ride and it's not smart to leave them lying around the lounge chairs. The alternative is to lock everything in a locker, but then how do you pay for something when you're hungry? Dollywood's Splash Country has solved that problem with Sunny Munny.

Sunny Munny is a wristband that can be purchased in the park. The wristbands come in either $25 or $50 amounts. Lock your valuables in a locker and wear the wristband around the park. When you want to pay for something, simply have the wristband scanned. Here's the best part: any unused money is refunded to you when you return the wristband. Sunny Munny can be purchased at the ticket counters outside the park and inside at Riverside Trading Post. You can buy more than one wristband if you think you will spend that much, but be advised, Sunny Munny is treated like cash. If you lose your wristband you will also lose the unused amount stored on it. This shouldn't be that much of a concern as the wristbands are quite secure.

RETREATS AND CANOPIES

Most water parks offer some sort of private space that can be rented while you enjoy the park. At Dollywood's Splash Country these are called retreats and canopies.

A canopy is sixty-five covered square feet with two lounge chairs. They are scattered throughout the park and can accommodate two people. Included in each canopy is a lockable storage bin. Canopies cost $50 for the whole day or $44 if you have a gold pass. Reservations are not required, but I highly recommend them because they fill up quickly. You can make a reservation for any date in the summer, usually starting in mid-April. Reservations can be made online at dollywood.com. Before you reserve a canopy you should download a map of their locations. The online reservation system will allow you to reserve a specific canopy.

Retreats use the same reservation system but are larger and more expensive. Retreats cost $190 or $170 for gold pass holders. These large spaces can hold up to twelve people and have two hundred covered square feet with a hundred square feet of sun deck. They also include a satellite television, ceiling fan, large table with chairs, lounge chairs, and lockable storage. There is a phone in the retreat to order food and have it brought to you. Retreats can, and should, be reserved online well in advance of your visit.

Dollywood's Splash Country also offers a few luxurious Deluxe Retreats. These are same as the regular retreats, except that they are a bit larger and include a couch, refrigerator with water, and bar stool seating. The Deluxe Retreats cost $300 per day or $280 for gold pass holders.

Massages are available in the retreats and canopies. Licensed therapists provide the service for guests that are eighteen or older. A sixty-minute Swedish massage is $120, or $96 if you have a gold pass. Reservations for massages are required at least twenty-four hours in advance; call 1-865-428-9488 to make an appointment.

If you make an online reservation for a retreat or canopy, your credit card will be used to hold the reservation. You must cancel by 72 hours of your date for a full refund. When you arrive at the park on the day of your reservation, report to the hospitality check-in desk located near the park entrance.

Again, the big question: is it worth it? This really depends upon the composition of your group. If it's a group entirely of active teenagers, then you can probably skip the option. However, as someone who likes to relax, it sure is nice to have guaranteed shade without the worry of having to run and save some lounge chairs early in the morning. For just me and my niece or nephews, a canopy is a great place to hang out. But, if you have any nonswimmers, a retreat can be heaven. When my parents are with us, they enjoy watching the kids and relaxing while being able to sit comfortably.

Butterfly Wisdom

Please don't get the idea that I have endless funds to spend on theme parks, gold passes, and retreats. My family puts traveling together as our number one priority and we budget accordingly. A good example of this is how we do Christmas.

If we know we are going to Dollywood's Splash Country the following summer, my sisters and I will always give my Dad a retreat reservation for his Christmas gift. To make it festive, we wrap a big box with a photo of a retreat. We all have too many material things in our lives and we feel that making memories is a great gift. Attraction tickets and gift cards for gas are also fantastic gifts for travelers.

Plus, there is a huge added benefit of giving summer memories as a Christmas gift. For the kids, it gives them six months of anticipation and dreams. I love thinking about my next trip because it gives me something to work toward. Kids love thinking and dreaming about the things they will do on vacation. Giving kids theme park tickets for Christmas gives them something to look forward to on those cold winter school days.

ATTRACTIONS AT DOLLYWOOD'S SPLASH COUNTRY

Now that we have all the essentials out of the way, it's time to focus on the main event: the attractions! There's a lot to do here and I will describe it all for you. However, Dollywood's Splash Country is entirely themed as a Smoky Mountain adventure. There are no separate theme park lands here. Because you're most likely to have a home base, I'll describe the attractions in the order they usually appear on the official park map. Remember, put on plenty of sunblock, stay hydrated, and let's get wet!

BEAR MOUNTAIN FIRE TOWER

Bear Mountain Fire Tower is a multi-level splash-pad that is a great place for younger guests to explore with their parents. There's a lot of water shooting everywhere and it's fun to use the interactive cannons to get others wet. Several smaller slides are attached to the main play structure. Nothing is too intense here.

The highlight of Bear Mountain is a thousand-gallon bucket attached at the very top. The bucket is slowly filled with water. Periodically, an alarm sounds and the bucket tips, spilling all one thousand gallons onto the people below. Children love the sensation of the deluge pouring on them and once is never enough.

BIG BEAR PLUNGE

This family raft ride sends groups of four down a large slide. Riders are sent through a number of tunnels as the rafts curve up and down the sides of the slide. Even though the park labels it as a family ride, it's not quite for the entire family. You must be at least thirty-six inches tall to ride. The plunge requires a climb up several flights of stairs and this ride is not accessible by those with disabilities.

DOWNBOUND FLOAT TRIP

Dollywood's Splash Country's version of a lazy river is not to be missed. Gently curving through the park past trees and hills, the river is 1,500 feet of calm current. There is only one entrance point that is located near the Riverside Trading Post. Plenty of tubes are available either already floating in the stream or lying aside the entrance. The ride begins with a beach-type entry that gently slopes into the water.

There is one area of beautifully cascading waterfalls that splash into the river. This is really the only place where you might get your hair wet if you are not careful. Otherwise, it is possible to float around and stay mostly dry above the neck. As with all lazy river rides, there are special rules about what you can and cannot do while floating. Many lifeguards are stationed around the river and will remind you of any rules. Also, one entrance means there is only one exit. Once on the river, you are committed to floating all the way around—about 15 minutes.

FIRE TOWER FALLS

Themed like a platform to look for fire in the Smoky Mountains, these two body slides are the fastest at the park. The slides stand seventy feet tall and are open to the elements. Riders free fall down the slides and naturally slow at the bottom due to long deceleration lanes. Fire Tower Falls requires a climb to the top and is not disability accessible.

LITTLE CREEK FALLS

Little Creek Falls is another area for younger guests. However, this attraction has a bigger pool and less interactive play structure. There are a few slides here that are a bit more intense than those at Bear Mountain.

The seating area around Little Creek Falls is popular with families. It is close to a play area, surrounded by the lazy river, and very near bathhouses and food options. Several colorful butterfly shades protect the lounge chairs from the sun.

MOUNTAIN SCREAM

Mountain Scream contains three slides grouped together. All three slides are body slides and you can choose which one you want while on the top platform. The middle option is an uncovered speed slide with four drops. On either side, you can find identical covered corkscrew-type twisting slides. These slides are a great example of the park's use of the natural hill. A climb is required and Mountain Scream is not accessible to those with disabilities.

MOUNTAIN TWIST

Located adjacent to Mountain Scream, Mountain Twist is also a combination of three slides. However, these are mat slides that require the use of a mat provided at the entrance. These slides are open and contain several curves. Some people have a preference as to which of the three is better, but you can do your own research and let those around you know. Mountain Twist, like its neighbor, requires a climb and is not disability accessible.

MOUNTAIN WAVES

It's impossible to miss the sprawling Mountain Waves pool in the middle of Dollywood's Splash Country. The surface area of the water measures 25,000 square feet. This wave pool progresses from a beach entry to a depth of six feet near the back wall. After a rest period of tranquility, the alarm sounds and the mountain begins to generate large waves.

You can swim freely, or use a tube inside the pool. There are several lifeguards that will be very attentive when the waves are present. It's a wild time and expect to bump into lots of tubes and arms while you brave the surf.

The area around Mountain Waves is the most popular place for people to set up their home base. Mostly in the sun, there are a couple of shelters that you might get to use if you are there early enough to grab one. Several beverage and snack vendors are located near the wave pool.

Every Friday in July the wave pool becomes host to the Splash Down Pool Party. A live DJ provides music for the Mountain Waves area. The music is a bit wilder when the waves are present and that makes the whole experience even better.

RAGING RIVER RAPIDS

Located near Mountain Twist, Raging River Rapids is the second of the park's family raft rides. Fairly similar to Big Bear Plunge, this ride also sends groups of rafters down a wide course. The one exception being that Raging River Rapids can hold five guests at one time, while Big Bear holds four. There is a maximum weight of eight hundred pounds per raft. Your group is weighed before you board, but don't worry, none of the weights are made known. However, your group may be asked to split apart if you exceed the weight. This ride is not disability accessible as a climb is required.

RIVERRUSH

This is the most popular and anticipated ride ever at Dollywood's Splash Country. RiverRush was the first hydromagnetic water coaster in the southeastern part of the United States. What's a hydromagnetic water coaster? Well, traditionally water rides went only in one direction because water flows in only one direction... down. That pesky gravity always gets in the way of fun. Thankfully, someone figured out that by placing induction motors along the track, and large magnets in each raft, you can make water seem to flow uphill. So, the water coaster was born and parks scrambled to get them.

RiverRush debuted in 2013 to very long lines. 2014 saw similarly long lines and the trend seems to continue; visit this attraction very early or very late and try to avoid it on weekends. Is it worth the wait? Yes! This water coaster is designed well and includes many sharp turns and several drops. There are multiple tunnels on the slide and the ride is long enough to justify the wait.

Four people can ride together on the toboggan-style raft. However, even hydromagnets have their limitations and each group must weigh less than seven hundred pounds. Again, your party will be weighed, but nobody will know the numbers. A conveyer belt lifts your raft up the first hill, and the rest is soaking wet history. One of the best aspects of RiverRush: there is no climb involved and the ride is completely accessible!

SLICK ROCK RACER

This slide, high on a hill, has four lanes that are easily spotted throughout the park. Each lane is identical and riders use mats, available at the entrance, to race each other to the bottom. The slide is open and can handle four racers at a time. Alas, there is no prize for winning, except perhaps making your little brother feel bad—and that just might be priceless. Both Slick Rock Racer and SwiftWater Run require a climb and are not accessible to those with disabilities.

SWIFTWATER RUN

My nephews always refer to this type of water slide as the toilet bowl...I suspect many of you do the same. Basically, you ride on a tube through a covered slide that drops you into an open bowl. You sort of swirl with the water around the bowl and plunge through a hole at the bottom. You can ride alone or with one other person. This ride runs backward at Dollywood's Australian AdventurePark in Sydney.

TAILSPIN RACER

New in 2017, TailSpin Racer is not visible from anywhere inside the park. As you enter Dollywood's Splash Country and approach the first group of buildings, look for the path on your left—it is marked with a sign.

TailSpin Racer is a racing lane water slide. This type of attraction has been added to most larger water parks during the past two years. Dollywood's version includes six lanes that begin at a height of five stories. Six racers are simultaneously sent careening down the slide on mats. Each of the lanes includes a tunnel and several curves.

As for the racing part—each lane is the same length and utilizes an equal force of water. Now, with that said, there are those that will swear one lane is faster than the others. I don't believe this has been scientifically proven because I've seen guests win from any of the lanes. There is no prize for the fastest slider; just relax and have a great time. (Of course, if you do win, it is always okay to rub-it-in a little.)

TailSpin Racer requires a climb and may not be accessible to those with disabilities.

THE BUTTERFLY

Situated near the middle of the park is this charming slide. Two tame body slides splash riders into a butterfly-shaped pool. It's fun to ride at least once for the novelty of sliding into a butterfly, but even most young kids think it's a bit too boring. However, the pool offers an excellent meeting spot. If you have to split up with your party, just tell them, "Meet me at the butterfly pool." They will know exactly where to find you. Unfortunately, there are a few steps involved and The Butterfly is not disability accessible.

THE CASCADES

This is the best themed area at Dollywood's Splash Country and probably my favorite place to swim. The Cascades is a very large swimming pool suitable for all ages. This is the second favorite spot for families to call home base because of the ample seating. Aside from being a gigantic pool, The Cascades has a number of nice waterfalls, a couple of small slides, and some interactive elements for small kids.

If you are tired of slides, done with a river tube, and just want to relax in water, The Cascades is your best option at the park. However, the area is quite exposed, so be sure to wear sunscreen.

WILD RIVER FALLS

Sitting near the park entrance and above the lazy river, you will notice the colorful tubes of Wild River Falls. These are a set of four slides that all contain curves as they drop you into a pool below. Two of the slides are completely enclosed and two have only partial tunnels. You can ride in a single or double tube. A climb is required and Wild River Falls is not disability accessible.

FOOD, SNACKS, AND BEVERAGES

FILL AND CHILL REFILLABLE MUGS

Dollywood's Splash Country has a refillable mug program that operates differently than the program at Dollywood. Here, the initial mug purchase is more expensive, but all the refills are free. A one-day Fill and Chill Refillable Mug is $15.99. A mug that can be refilled for free all season long is $25. Gold pass discounts are available.

There are multiple Fill and Chill stations located around the park that offer many varieties of sodas, lemonades, and teas. In order to stop families from purchasing one mug and filling it many times for several people, there is a ten-minute waiting period between each refill. The Fill and Chill locations are marked with a cup and straw on the park map. (Note: Hosts will allow guests to use their refillable Dollywood mug for a cost of $1.)

BEAVER TAILS 🍽

These treats are so good that they seem to come directly from Satan. In actuality, they are imports from Canada where Beaver Tails is a large chain. And, in the largest theme park coup of the century, this location at Dollywood's Splash Country was the first Beaver Tails establishment in the entire United States.

What's a beaver tail and what makes them so good? Well, basically, wholewheat dough is stretched into the shape of a beaver tail and fried. You could just eat the fried dough—but who in their right mind would ever do that? There are several topping to choose from, including: chocolate, peanut butter, various types of candy bars, others types of candy, and cinnamon sugar. The toppings are added to the beaver tail while it is still warm and, as you can imagine, an irresistible treat is served.

My grandpa, before he left us to visit that big theme park in the sky, used to say, "I could put that much sugar on a dishrag and it would taste just the same." Grandpa was probably right—but fried dough makes a great alternative.

BERRIES AND CREAM 🍽

All sorts of ice cream products are available here. Milkshakes, ice cream bowls, floats, sundaes, and soft-serve are offered. Of course, fresh berries and ice cream can be mixed to create their namesake dessert.

CAMPSITE GRILL

The largest and most diverse restaurant in the park, Campsite Grill offers all the theme park fare you can imagine. Burgers, fries, chicken, wraps, and croissant sandwiches are made fresh in front of you. There are shaded tables available around the outside of the restaurant for you to use. Unlike the buffets and formal restaurants of Dollywood, here at Dollywood's Splash Country, all food is offered quick-service style.

CASCADES CONCESSIONS

Located in the back of the park near The Cascades, this vendor sells mainly the Dipping Dots brand of ice cream. There is a refrigerator of premade salads, wraps, and subs to serve those that don't want to walk across the park. This vendor also stocks sunglasses and sunscreen.

DOGS-N-TATORS

Almost identical to the restaurant of the same name over at Dollywood, Dogs-N-Tators sells freshly made corn dogs and those piles of potato swirls. There is a Fill and Chill location next door and a patio with tables.

GRAB AND GO

A quick place to get a snack, Grab and Go has a number of coolers that you open and take what you like. There are beverages, wraps, and containers of ice cream.

HIGH COUNTRY PROVISIONS

Located near the wave pool, High Country Provisions is a snacker's paradise. Nachos, tacos, chili dogs, and potato chips with all sorts of toppings are offered.

MISS MAMIE'S PIZZA 🍽

Pizza and breadsticks are the items of choice at this location. The freshly made pizzas are sold in small personal-sized pies. This is a larger restaurant that also has nearby tables with umbrellas.

MOUNTAIN WAVES HYDRATION STATION 🍽

Here, you can purchase a cup and fill it with several varieties of slushies. You can even mix the flavors if you like.

OUTPOST SNACKS 🍽

Also near the wave-pool, Outpost Snacks offers barbeque sandwiches and hot-dogs.

THE WATERING HOLE 🍽

You can find soft drinks and all sorts of snacks here. Cotton candy, cookies, and large pretzels are sold.

SHOPS

There are a lot of differences between a standard theme park and a water park, but none more than the availability of shopping. For some reason, people prefer to be fully clothed while they shop. While Dollywood has countless shopping opportunities, Dollywood's Splash Country really has just two stores.

RIVERSIDE TRADING POST 🛍

This is the larger of the two shops and is located toward the front of the park. As you might imagine, swimwear dominates the store. There are many styles in all sizes for men, women, and children.

There is also a large selection of beach towels and sunscreen. Riverside Trading Post is the best place to purchase Dollywood's Splash Country souvenir items including t-shirts.

SPLASH AND DASH SUNDRIES

A smaller shop located more toward the center of the park, Splash and Dash Sundries sells sunglasses, towels, and sunscreen. There is also a freezer with ready-made ice cream novelties for sale. I hate to mention it, because I find them a bit annoying, but Splash and Dash is the place to buy a Big Squirt.

Big Squirt is basically a nozzle attached to a compression hose. While you hold the gadget below water and pull out the compression hose, water is taken into the Big Squirt. Then, when you raise the gadget out of the water, the compression hose contracts and creates enough pressure to spray the water out from the nozzle. Go ahead and squirt to your heart's content inside the pools. However, out of the pools, please be considerate of those around you. Believe it or not, there are times when all of us have had enough water and want to remain in the park, but also want to stay dry.

So, that's Dollywood's Splash Country! Swim until the cows come home, or until your hands are so wrinkly that you look like an alien. Don't forget to find some time to sit and relax in the beautiful mountain setting.

When you're ready to leave, make a final check to see that you've got everything and make your way toward the exit. Surprisingly, you exit through the same gate that you entered—no exit through the gift shop here! While you find the way back to your car, take a moment and look at your traveling companions. Notice how normal their skin looks and pause to thank me, and yourself, for using sunscreen. Now, go shower and have a sunburn-free night of sleep!

CHAPTER 5

EVENTS AND FESTIVALS

No matter which part of the operating season you choose to visit Dollywood, you will most likely be part of some sort of festival. Most theme parks realize that holding festivals is a good way to encourage people to make multiple visits during various seasons of the year. However, at Dollywood, the festivals are much more related to music and performing arts than festivals in other parks. For example, you won't find Happy Dolloween in October or Merry Jinglewood in December. Instead, you will discover festivals that are based on the food and music of the season without the types of things you may see at your local mall.

Special events and festivals do not just occur inside the butterfly gates. The surrounding tourist towns offer plenty of activities that change seasonally. Pigeon Forge's Old Mill Heritage Day and Gatlinburg's famous midnight Fourth of July Parade are two examples of annual events. Since these cities change their calendars and events often, I will only focus on Dollywood festivals in this chapter. To find more information on neighboring events, please visit:
- Sevierville at visitsevierville.com
- Pigeon Forge at mypigeonforge.com
- Gatlinburg at gatlinburg.com

At Dollywood, festivals do not incur any additional charges for nonfood related events. Regular admission is all you need to enjoy the extra shows, exhibits, decorations, and fireworks. Of course, if you decide to eat some of the special dining offerings, you will pay extra. However, you have to eat no matter what time of year and special event food is never priced any higher than the regular Dollywood fare.

DOLLYWOOD'S FESTIVAL OF NATIONS

For a theme park with a large emphasis on American patriotism, it might be surprising to learn of the enormous production that is the Festival of Nations. A lot of credit is due to Dollywood planners that realize the importance of bringing the world to the Smoky Mountains. For many Dollywood visitors, an actual journey across the ocean is far too expensive and time consuming. Dollywood goes to great lengths to entertain and educate all of us about the world we live in.

Usually starting on Dollywood opening weekend and continuing through most of April, Festival of Nations brings performance groups from many countries to the park. In 2019, twenty different countries were represented with twenty different performance groups. The amount of shows available during this time of year is staggering. You will certainly want to download the show schedule from dollywood.com and plan your day before your arrival.

The countries and performance groups change every year. In the past, shows have included:
- an extravaganza of African dancing, drumming, and acrobatics
- a dance troupe from Colombia
- a Russian folk trio
- a group of Swiss yodelers and alphorn players
- a renowned pianist from Italy
- one of the world's best harpists, sent from Paraguay

- Canadian singers that are very famous in their own country, but who we've never heard of before
- acrobats from China
- native people of Incan descent with authentic instruments
- stilt dancers from Bavaria
- bagpipers from Scotland

The range and diversity of our planet is extraordinary. Nothing demonstrates that more than *Dollywood's One World Celebration*. Occurring daily during the festival, all the performers from the various groups dance with park guests in a gigantic street bash. The celebration takes place on Showstreet and is sure to be the most colorful musical event you've ever seen.

One thing common to all the world: we need to eat. How we eat may differ greatly, but delicious food comes from every corner of the globe. Dollywood's World Passport to Food brings dishes from around the world to the park during the Festival of Nations. Check the special park brochure, or dollywood.com before your visit to see this year's menu. Most of this special food is available from stands placed along Showstreet and Market Square.

FLOWER AND FOOD FESTIVAL

There is no denying that in the theme park business, Disney is top dog—er—mouse. The Disney Parks are so much larger that even their closest competitor that everything they do trickles down throughout the industry. Some years ago, Disney had the brilliant idea of holding a festival centered around food and gardening at Epcot. They already had the gardens and they could make money from selling the special food. It was a huge success that continues to this day.

Dollywood followed suit with its own Flower and Food Festival. I consider this to be a fairly minor event compared to the park's other seasonal extravaganzas. Dollywood always has amazing food and beautiful landscaping—this festival augments those aspects of the park. Like Disney, Dollywood uses this festival as a way to advertise to the local residents during a time of the year when traditional tourists aren't traveling as much. It's a smart business move.

A few large topiaries and a delightful canopy of umbrellas are the featured elements of this festival. The topiaries are spread throughout the park and represent Smoky Mountain life, including one of Dolly's mother sewing her famous coat. The umbrella canopy is on Showstreet along with various stands that offer spring-related foods. The Flower and Food Festival overlaps a bit with the Barbecue and Bluegrass event.

BARBEQUE AND BLUEGRASS

Taking place from around Memorial Day and through the first week of June, the Barbeque and Bluegrass Festival brings the best of both those Southern staples to Dollywood.

Outside of Vince Gill, I'm not too knowledgeable about bluegrass, but I'm told that Dollywood's festival brings the best of the best to the park. Bluegrass aficionados will recognize all the names that change yearly. The shows occur inside the park's various theaters. You can find an entire schedule on dollywood.com, usually early May.

For the second half of the festival, head to Market Square between Showstreet and Rivertown Junction for the barbeque feast. You will be able to smell it long before you see it. There are all sorts of meats including pulled pork, chicken, beef, and, of course, ribs. You can select from several sauces, some of which are quite spicy. There are also plenty of special desserts around.

SUMMER CELEBRATION

Occurring when most of the nation's schools are on break, Great American Summer begins the second week of June and continues through the first week of August. Aside from the Imagination Playhouse in The Village, there are two other big advantages of visiting Dollywood during this time.

First, Great American Summer offers the longest operating day of the park's calendar. Dollywood is open from 10 a.m. to 10 p.m. every single day during the festival. Other times of the year, the park can close as early as 6pm and open as late as 2pm. Families will enjoy the extra time in the park. For me, theme parks at night are just that much more magical. The Country Fair looks more real with its carnival lights aglow. The dim lanterns of Craftsman's Valley make it easier for me to be immersed in the theme.

Second, everyday of Great American Summer ends with a bang. What says "American" and "summer" more than fireworks? *Dolly's Nights of Many Colors* occurs each night, usually around 9:45 p.m. The official start time is listed in the daily show schedule. The impressive display is coordinated to several of Dolly's greatest hits. She also composed a new song for the show and there is a fitting patriotic finale.

There are several great spots to view and listen to the fireworks extravaganza. The most popular spot is in front of the Dollywood Emporium on Showstreet. People prefer this location because a quick exit can be made through the emporium when the show is over. A number of people also congregate in the back of the park near the Wild Eagle coaster. This location requires a longer walk when the show is over, but the darkness back here makes for better viewing. I prefer to watch from the middle of Adventures in Imagination. There is never a crowd and the sound system is easy to hear. Also, there is something special about seeing the fireworks explode over the area of the park that I call its "soul." Still, some people swear that the best location to see the fireworks is back in parking lot F. I've never seen the show from there, so I can't vouch for it, but I've been told the darkness and elevation make for a spectacular show. However, please note that if you choose parking lot F you won't be able to hear the coordinated music.

If you are a guest at Dollywood's DreamMore Resort you can see the fireworks well from the hotel's back porch on the second level. You won't be able to hear the music, but the show is still fun to watch. If you're not a guest at the resort you can still watch the fireworks from the back porch by visiting the hotel's restaurant for dinner and sticking around.

Regardless of where you stand, *Dolly's Nights of Many Colors* is worth a visit at least once during your vacation.

Butterfly Wisdom

Visiting a theme park, any theme park, is always a delicate balance of expectations and disappointments. It's difficult to manage because you want to be excited for your trip by researching what you want to do. However, knowing what you want can easily lead to disappointment if it doesn't happen. I try to convince myself that just being in the park is the best part and everything I get to do is a bonus. However, it's easy for me to think that way because I've been there before and I'm not a kid.

When we travel to a theme park with kids, I always give them the "we're just going to be happy to be there and we're not going to cry" speech. I make up situations and get them to join me on the catch phrase.

"So, what happens if it starts to rain and the fireworks are canceled?" I ask.

"We're just going to be happy to be there and we're not going to cry," they respond in a robotic monotone.

"What if the Wild Eagle is down for maintenance?"

"We're just going to be happy to be there and we're not going to cry. We get it."

This might sound like a stupid tactic, but it works. If it actually does start to rain before the fireworks, one of the kids will say the phrase in an obnoxious voice, the others will laugh and somehow, everything seems okay.

HARVEST FESTIVAL

Beginning the last week of September and continuing until the last week of October, this festival is one of the premier events for gospel music in the United States. There are really three parts to this festival: the concerts, the crafters, and the decorations.

The gospel concerts are all over the entire park. For the 2019 festival, I counted eighty-nine different gospel groups. There are solo acts, quartets, and everything you can imagine including entire choirs. All concerts are free with Dollywood admission. The calendar of the concerts is posted in late summer. Obviously, not all eighty-nine groups can be there everyday. The schedule will list the groups and the dates they will perform. You will have to wait until the week before your visit to download a schedule of the exact times for performances.

Want even more handmade items at Dollywood? The Harvest Festival also includes a craft fair. Crafters from all over the country make Dollywood their home during the fall. Once again, you can check dollywood.com in late summer to see which crafters will be there during which times. Unlike the gospel performers, the crafters tend to be at the park each operating day for long periods of time. Most of these artisans live in an RV parked somewhere near the park and see this festival as a way to vacation and make money. In fact, Dollywood is always looking for new crafters and you can easily apply on dollywood.com. The crafters are diverse and make anything you can imagine, including: Christmas ornaments, dolls, jewelry, musical instruments, baskets, rugs, paintings, dishware, and many other items. And, as part of their contract with the park, all crafters have agreed to demonstrate their craft and interact with guests.

Lastly, the Harvest Festival includes incredible decor. If you visited Dollywood in the summer, you won't believe it's the same park with fall colors everywhere. Of course, the natural colors of the mountains provide a spectacular backdrop for the park's pumpkins, scarecrows, and gourds galore. There are enough pumpkins at Dollywood alone to keep several pumpkin patches in business.

Speaking of the fall harvest, one October day I saw a Dollywood host picking up a couple of leaves that had fallen on the pavement in Timber Canyon. It never occurred to me that all of those thousands of trees in the park have millions of leaves—many of which fall onto the pristine pavement. As I've said before, Dollywood was not fabricated on an empty slate from the ground up. Instead, the park has been built through and around hills and forests. I love this about the park. But now, one of the things I love about Dollywood was showing a negative side.

So I asked the Dollywood host about all the leaves and how they keep the park clean. She replied that it all has to do with staying ahead of the trees. Every night in the fall, even if the park was not open that day, Dollywood hosts use machines to clean off all the walkways. Then, during the day, several hosts roam the park and pick up any stray leaves they see. This same process also occurs at Dollywood's Splash Country, even though that park is closed for the season. The leaves are composted and reused in both theme parks and the resort. Without this massive undertaking, a walk through the sparkling world of a Dollywood Christmas would be a sloppy, dirty mess.

Please note: If you visit the Harvest Festival in October, you will get two festivals for the price of one. Keep reading...

GREAT PUMPKIN LUMINIGHTS

New in 2017, and so successful that it instantly became a tradition, Great Pumpkin LumiNights delights guests from the last weekend of September through the first weekend after Halloween. Dollywood is open late each night of the event because the pumpkins are better viewed after the sun goes down. 4,000 carved pumpkins line the paths from Showstreet, up to Timber Canyon, and through to Wilderness Pass. The pumpkins are lit with flameless candles and glow in all their eerie splendor.

While walking through the LumiNights, it's important to look around and up. There are lit pumpkins carved like owls and bats hanging in the trees. A large creepy spider, entirely of carved pumpkins, joins other large characters. Most of the pumpkins are real and are joined by large artificial guards to complete the look.

Master pumpkin carvers occupy a cabin near the entrance to the Thunderhead coaster. These artisans are incredible and carve all sorts of images into pumpkins. They use various instruments to carve different layers in the pumpkin's shell. When lit, the results are beautiful and mysterious. I wish I could do this back home. Feel free to linger here and ask the carvers any questions you may have.

Near the beginning of Wilderness Pass, at the Wilderness Plaza, you can find the giant Great Pumpkin Tree. This tree, made of sculpted faux jack-o-lanterns, glows with subdued beauty. Atmospheric music sets the perfect mood in this area. During the day, the tree makes a fantastic photo spot. At night, Dollywood photographers are in the area to snap a perfect photo with their advanced cameras. There is usually a costumed pumpkin mascot nearby that can be included in your pose.

Several fall-themed characters roam the LumiNights. There is some sort of large man made of pumpkin vines and another dressed as a large owl. They are joined by a roving jack-o-lantern and ultra-cute scarecrow. Dollywood photographers are on hand to snap a photo for your social media profile.

In addition to all this autumnal atmosphere, Dollywood offers special foods and merchandise during Great Pumpkin LumiNights. Pumpkin funnel cake, candy corn cotton candy, friend apple pies, pumpkin cookies, pumpkin lattes, caramel apple sundaes, and pumpkin bread are a few of the treats available throughout the park. The Dollywood Emporium stocks T-shirts, mugs, and other souvenirs that are themed to the event.

During this festival, timing can be important depending upon the type of experience you want. Early in October the crowds are considerably lower and the pumpkin carvings are all fresh. Later in October you will notice that some of the pumpkins have begun to wilt a bit. Also, crowds grow the closer the calendar gets to October 31st. However, for those of you that love fall colors on the trees, the peak time for fall foliage in the Smoky Mountains tends to be late October or even early November. Expect large crowds if you visit during the evening on weekends.

We all know that Linus was wasting his time in that pumpkin patch with Sally and Snoopy. He should have visited Dollywood's Great Pumpkin LumiNights. With all sincerity, he would surely have seen the Great Pumpkin.

SMOKY MOUNTAIN CHRISTMAS

We've covered the rest, now let's talk about the best. The entire park is closed the first week of November while Dollywood and its army of workers prepare for the most unbelievable spectacle in the Smokies. Not even the Grinch could steal Christmas at Dollywood because he'd have no idea where to start. Neither will you.

First, there are the special holiday shows in each of the theaters. I've already covered these shows in Chapter 3. Just let me remind you that the Christmas shows are no afterthought to give the park an excuse to remain open in December. These shows are full-fledged, elaborate productions with all the musicians, sets, and costumes you'd expect in New York. They are also quite crowded and you should arrive early to get a seat for any live musical experience during Dollywood's Smoky Mountain Christmas. Remember to consider TimeSaver, or grab show vouchers from the hosts if they are offered.

I also covered the holiday menus in Chapter 3, as well as the special Santa's Workshop in the Country Fair and Rudolph's Holly Jolly Junction in Craftsman's Valley. However, there are a few things I didn't mention yet.

Dolly's Parade of Many Colors, introduced in 2016, takes place once or twice each night during Smoky Mountain Christmas. Christmas floats made of thousands of lights gracefully float from Heartsong Theater, through Showstreet to the gazebo, and into Adventures in Imagination. Check the show schedule for the parade time. Park hosts will draw a system of chalk barriers on the pavement; anywhere near these lines is a good place to stand. The Dollywood hosts seem to have as much fun as the guests during this parade as they get to portray lots of fun characters.

This elaborate multi-million dollar spectacle begins with Santa Claus riding an illuminated train. He is followed by brilliantly lit gingerbread houses, large gifts, and, of course, butterflies. My favorite float is a fantastic guitar with glowing strings that keep time with the parade's soundtrack. The parade concludes with an unbelievable series of floats dedicated to the nativity.

Dolly's Parade of Many Colors pays homage to Dolly's famous song and the holiday movie that it inspired. Look for the patchwork pieces that comprised little Dolly's coat—you will find this patchwork pattern on most floats and as part of the costumes of those in the parade. Even though this parade could just have easily been called *Dolly's Parade of Many Spectators*, there is plenty of room for everyone to stand along the route. However, be advised that most people leave the park after the parade in one giant mass exodus. My tip: stay inside Dollywood and take in the fabulous atmosphere—linger slowly and exit after all the great horde has departed.

Shows, parades, and food are nice, but, believe it or not, they are not the main draw. The true star of Dollywood's Smoky Mountain Christmas is the spectacle of 6 million Christmas lights attached to anything that doesn't move. I truly think that if you stand still long enough, some Dollywood host is going to cover you with lights. There is not one building in the park that isn't outlined or completely filled-in with light. Showstreet is especially amazing. Also, make sure to look for one of the four feature trees of the park. While all the trees have lights strung around them, four special trees have all their branches individually wrapped with lights. It's hard to explain, but imagine taking yarn and wrapping it around each branch of a tree—all the way to its smallest part. Then, make the yarn glow. That's what these trees are like. Why only four feature trees? It takes five days for teams of three people to wrap each tree. And, if you've had too much of the refillable hot chocolate and need to use the facilities, head to The Village. Next to Heartsong Theater you will find the most Christmas-lit restrooms in North America, probably the world!

The largest spectacles, and awesome photo spots, for Smoky Mountain Christmas are the two giant trees toward the back of the park. The Wildwood Tree back in Wildwood Grove is always there, but it's extra special at Christmas with the colors and songs of the season. But the biggest tree in the park is the technological wonder of Wilderness Plaza. This tree is only here at Christmas and is comprised of several large LED screens. The screens of light are choreographed to the music that is played throughout the plaza. Hot chocolate is available for purchase nearby and you can easily spend an entire evening just in this one spot.

The giant tree of Wilderness Plaza signals the beginning of Glacier Ridge. During Smoky Mountain Christmas, the entire area from Wilderness Pass through to Craftsman's Valley becomes an amazing journey of blue and white lights. Using light to mimic ice, Glacier Ridge is full of Arctic sights, including adorable polar bears. Wonderful illuminated snowflakes hang above all the strolling guests. Be sure not to miss the Arctic Passage, a large tunnel of calming lights. And, yes, for those of you like my roller-coaster obsessed nephew, all the non-water rides are open in Glacier Ridge including Wild Eagle and FireChaser Express.

The sheer number of lights and their perfectly placed bulbs are impossible to describe. There really is nothing else like it in the world. I frequent the Disney Parks during the holidays—they are amazing and tastefully decorated to the nines. However, Dollywood has that "over-the-top" feeling that reminds me of my childhood. Dollywood's light display is more Clark Griswold than it is Martha Stewart.

Butterfly Wisdom

I'll let you in on my personal secret viewing location—as long as you promise not to tell too many others. Head to Rivertown Junction and climb the steep hill behind Aunt Granny's Restaurant. Look for Rainbow Blown Glass Factory. Directly across from the factory is a green park bench. From this place, look all around you and take in the site of millions of Christmas lights shining from nearby Rivertown Junction and The Village. There is hardly ever other people hanging out in this part of the park and you will have a few solitary moments to reflect on the beauty.

Listen for the soothing sounds of orchestral carols coming from the junction below. Stay long enough to hear the whistle of the Dollywood Express with its load of holiday revelers. As you can tell, I enjoy the serenity, symbolism, and beauty of this particular place within Dollywood and cherish the few moments I am fortunate to spend there.

Along with the lights, expect crowds during Smoky Mountain Christmas. Weekends in December are the most crowded Dollywood attendance days of the entire year! I visited one Saturday night in December and had to park in Dollywood's Splash Country parking lot. Fortunately, most people visit to look at the lights and lines for attractions are surprisingly short (excluding the shows). To avoid crowds, go during the week or before Thanksgiving. During Smoky Mountain Christmas, Dollywood is normally closed on Mondays, Tuesdays, and some Wednesdays. The park is closed Christmas Eve, Christmas Day, and New Year's Eve. Dollywood is open on New Year's Day, Thanksgiving, and Black Friday. (It's a much better option than shopping; probably a better deal too!)

Light the Way 5K is a special event that takes place annually the second Friday of November. The run/walk is a fantastic way to experience the park, and all its lights, well after dark. A fundraiser for the Dollywood Pay it Forward Foundation and Keep Sevier Beautiful, the event costs $35 or $25 if you register before July 1. The race kicks off at 11pm and participants conquer the course that winds through the parking lots and through Dollywood. All of Dollywood's four millions lights are illuminate and sparkling for the runners/walkers. There is an awards ceremony following the race at the Showstreet Palace Theater, but don't worry about this event as a competitive race. Yes, some people in each age group will win, but the rest of us are just glad to walk, see the lights, and raise money for some worthy causes. Each participant gets a T-shirt, goody bag, and a light-up red Rudolph nose. The event has its own website at: lighttheway5k.net.

For several years Dollywood has offered a unique ticket opportunity involving Smoky Mountain Christmas. If you purchase a season pass for the next calendar year, you can attend Smoky Mountain Christmas for free during the current year. For example, if you buy a 2021 season pass in November of 2020, you can enter Dollywood as much as you want from your day of purchase through January 2022. Keep this deal in mind when you budget for your ticket needs. If you only enter Dollywood during Smoky Mountain Christmas, and you do this every year, you can essentially visit the festival as much as you want by purchasing one season pass just every two years. Be advised, this policy could change; make sure you confirm with a Dollywood host before your purchase.

Regardless of the ticket you use to enter the park, dress in layers as the weather is unpredictable. You won't want to miss a minute by being cold or wet. It's also a good idea to figure out how to take night photos with your camera.

Before we leave the most wonderful time of the year, and at the risk of sounding like a broken record, I need one more moment to praise the extravaganza that is Dollywood's Smoky Mountain Christmas. I am a Christmas junkie. I am not ashamed to admit that, for me, when the clock strikes midnight on October 31st my world magically changes from Halloween to Christmas. (Of course, I pause to stuff my face on Thanksgiving.) By November 3rd, my home looks like Mrs. Claus threw up all over the place; I love it!

I've been to all the Disney Parks around the world for their Christmas festivals. I've visited the great U.S. cities in all their holiday glory. I've been to all the major Christmas markets in Europe. There isn't a Hallmark Christmas movie that I haven't watched. I've seen more holiday decorations than are packed on the Grinch's sleigh. With all my Christmas experience, I am not afraid to recommend Dollywood's Smoky Mountain Christmas: It is truly the best Christmas event on the planet without exception.

MICHAEL'S DOLLYWOOD GINGERBREAD

Aside from writing, I love baking—especially at Christmas. This is a recipe for loaves of gingerbread that I've tinkered with over the years. You can use any brand of apple butter in this recipe, however, the bread tastes much better with Dollywood apple butter that you can purchase from the Emporium on Showstreet. There is a bit of Dolly Parton magic in every jar and that's why it tastes so good.

MICHAEL FRIDGEN

¾ cup room temperature butter

1½ cup sugar

1 teaspoon vanilla

2 eggs

1½ cup Dollywood apple butter

2¼ cup flour

1½ teaspoon baking soda

1 teaspoon baking powder

1 Tablespoon ground ginger

1 Tablespoon cinnamon

1½ teaspoon ground cloves

1 teaspoon nutmeg

1½ teaspoon salt

1. Using a mixer, combine the butter and sugar. Mix on a high speed until smooth.
2. Add the eggs, vanilla, and apple butter. Mix on a medium speed until well combined.
3. In a separate bowl, mix the remaining ingredients by hand.
4. Add the wet ingredients to the dry ingredients. Mix by hand until just combined; do not over mix.
5. Spray or grease 4 small loaf pans. I use 6 inch by 3 inch pans. This recipe does not bake well in a large pan.
6. Divide dough evenly and place in the prepared pans.
7. Bake in a pre-heated 350-degree oven for 30-40 minutes.
8. Allow to cool for 10 minutes and release loaves from the pans.
9. Enjoy with your family as you listen to the Dolly Parton and Kenny Rogers Christmas album.

CHAPTER 6

OUTSIDE DOLLY'S WORLD

Believe it or not, there are things to do in the area that have nothing to do with Dolly Parton. Great Smoky Mountain National Park for one. You could spend weeks in just the national park hiking, climbing, rafting, and picnicking. Then, there are music shows, museums, and historical markers all over the area, not to mention the outlet shopping, restaurants, and mountain crafters. The focus of this book is to present guidance for a visit to the Dollywood theme parks, but I'll give a brief description of some of the other attractions in this chapter.

DOLLY PARTON'S STAMPEDE

All right, so I lied a little bit. Dolly Parton's Stampede is owned by Dolly Parton and part of the Dollywood Company. But in my defense, it's located outside of Dolly's World on the main tourist strip in Pigeon Forge. Just south of the intersection of Parkway and Dollywood Lane, you can't miss the large dinner attraction with its huge parking lot and sparkling marquee.

Part rodeo, part Broadway show, and part grandma's kitchen, Dolly Parton's Stampede is a multi-faceted dinner attraction.

Ticket prices for the stampede change depending upon the time of year, time of performance, and how close you want to sit to the action. Adults should expect to pay around $48 and children are a bit cheaper. For your exact price visit dixiestampede.com. Please note, Dolly Parton's Stampede has two locations: one in Pigeon Forge and the other in Branson, Missouri; make sure you select the correct location. Regardless of the ticket you buy, dinner and show are included in the price.

Dolly Parton's Stampede in Pigeon Forge normally produces one or two performances each day. During the summer and busy Christmas season, they can perform as many as four performances in one day. The website will have the most current performance times. It's not uncommon for the attraction to add performances if they are sold out. If you can't get tickets and still want to attend, call Dolly Parton's Stampede at 865-453-4400 a day or two before to see if a show has been added.

When you purchase tickets, you'll be asked if you want to cheer for the North or for the South. The main arena show is a lively competition between riders from the North and riders from the South. It's the most fun if you can sit on the side where you actually live. But sometimes your side may sell-out and you'll have to root for the other team—just grin and bear it and your side may still win.

The time on your ticket is the time that your performance of the arena show will begin. However, there is more that happens before. Plan to arrive at least an hour before your printed show time. Your experience begins right in the parking lot where you can walk up to the building and see the real stars of the show...the magnificent horses of Dolly Parton's Stampede. (Oh yeah, there are horses—we'll get to that.)

Then, head inside and find your way to the Belle Saloon. In this large two-level venue, you'll have a chance to hear an opening act that is usually bluegrass in nature. This is also the only place where you can buy items not included with your ticket. Popcorn, peanuts, and soft drinks are available. There are also souvenir boot mugs of frozen drinks that are quite popular. (As with all Dollywood attractions, everything is nonalcoholic.) It's not a problem if you don't buy anything. There will be plenty of food and drink to come that is included with your ticket.

You'll clap, sing, and generally raise the roof in the saloon. Before you know it, the performers will announce that it's show time. Now, you'll follow the crowd into the large arena; the first sight of the space is always impressive. Your ticket will have an aisle and table number on it. Ushers will guide you to your place. Everyone in your party will be seated on a long bench with a table in front of it. You'll all be facing into the middle of the area. Don't worry that you can't see each other to talk because the show will start immediately.

Suddenly, out of nowhere, the arena will fill with horses and riders. An emcee will guide you through the evening's festivities. You'll cheer with your side of the arena as riders from the North and South compete in various tests of horsemanship. Between the competitions, different scenes of large production value are performed. These scenes change from year to year, but have included waltzing Southern Belles, strapping lumberjacks, and stampeding buffalo.

While you watch all of this, the hardest working servers in town will bring the feast to you. Your jar will never be empty as you drink unlimited soda, tea, or coffee. The feast begins with a creamy vegetable soup that you slurp from a bowl. Did I forget to mention that the only utensil available is a fork? Yep. Just dig right in and relax...you'll be given a large wet towel when the meal is complete. After the soup, the main feast is served. Both a whole rotisserie chicken and barbeque pork loin are the main entrees. On the side you will receive corn on the cob, an herb-basted potato and a biscuit. At some point all of this is cleared away—I'm usually too involved in the show to know when this happens. For dessert, you're served an apple turnover.

There is a vegetarian option of vegetable pasta available. Children are served the same meal as adults. Unfortunately, Dolly Parton's Stampede is not a place for those with animal-related allergies. The arena floor is dirt and dust gets into the air. Only you can judge the level of your allergy and decide if you can attend.

Now, back to the feast. After your dessert plate is cleared and you've got your towel, the show will come to a rousing climax as you discover which side wins. But again, there's nothing to worry about. No matter who wins, a patriotic finale reminds the crowd that despite our vast differences, we are part of the same country. And, just in case you don't believe that final message, Dolly appears via the sound system to remind you that we are all in this together. I can't imagine too many are going to argue with her.

It shouldn't surprise you that Christmas at Dolly Parton's Stampede is special and holiday-inspired. The preshow and format are the same, as is the feast, but the show is completely different. During Christmas, you'll cheer for either the North Pole Elves or South Pole Elves. Also, the scenes between the competitions are Christmas-based with lots of holiday costumes and Christmas carols. The climax of the Christmas show is a live nativity with real camels, sheep, donkeys, and flying angels. Of course, Santa and his sleigh are on hand as well as thousands of lights on all the horses and riders. It's quite a spectacle that is guaranteed to put you in the Christmas mood.

Overall, Dolly Parton's Stampede is a fantastic meal and over two hours of entertainment. It's not cheap for a family to attend, but when you consider the price of a movie these days, you're getting a lot of value for your money.

PIRATES VOYAGE DINNER & SHOW

I promise—this is the last Dolly Parton attraction that I'll write about. (Although, she probably opened two more since this book went to press.) Pirates Voyage Dinner & Show, located near The Island in Pigeon Forge, is a similar, but smaller, version of Dolly Parton's Stampede.

When guests arrive they are treated to appetizers and music in the theater's Pirates Village. At showtime, guests are seated at long tables that curve around three sides of the stage. There is really not a bad seat here.

Dinner includes Voyager Creamy Vegetable Soup, biscuits, fried chicken, pork chop, potatoes, mac 'n' cheese, and peach pie. Again, as with Dolly Parton's Stampede, there is a lot of food served here. It's best to eat a late breakfast and skip lunch if you plan on attending this show.

As you eat the show happens in front of you. Blackbeard and Calico Jack lead the rival Crimson and Sapphire pirate brigades as they battle their way through various stunts. The show includes a full-size pirate ship that sits in the middle of a water-filled lagoon. The action takes place all around: on the ship, in the water, and above in the air. You will also spot mermaids and birds while you dine.

Even pirates get into the Christmas spirit. During the holiday season, usually beginning the first week of November, Pirates Voyage Dinner & Show presents a Christmas twist. The whole place is decked out and dressed up for the season. The structure of the whole experience remains the same with special holiday touches showing up here and there. Just note: Blackbeard is clearly not on the Nice List.

Expect to pay around $45 for an adult ticket and $25 for a child. Again, it's not cheap for a family to attend. But you are guaranteed to be fed and entertained.

Butterfly Wisdom

If you arrive at Dollywood via Knoxville, and drive on I-40 through downtown Knoxville, you are sure to see a large gold disco ball sitting on top of a tower. That's the Sunsphere and was the symbol of the 1982 Knoxville World's Fair. Since the fair, the 266-foot structure has had an unstable history with various restaurants and bars opening and closing inside the observation decks. I'm not sure what you'd find if you decide to take a closer look on your drive, but the plaza around it can make a nice photograph. And, for those fans of The Simpsons television show, the Sunsphere was not really turned into the Wigsphere—a giant wig store Bart visited in 1996.

The history of theme parks is perpetually linked with the history of World's Fairs. The man who built the first theme park with lands, Walt Disney, had a fascination with World's Fairs and used them for inspiration several times. In fact, Walt's father was a construction foreman for the famous 1893 Chicago World's Fair that debuted the Ferris wheel. Walt went on to design several attractions for the 1964–1965 New York World's Fair. Great Moments with Mr. Lincoln, it's a small world, and the Carousel of Progress were among the attractions that Walt moved to Disneyland after the fair.

Disneyland wasn't the only theme park to inherit a ride from the New York World's Fair. After the fair, a log flume was dismantled and stored for a brief period. Art Modell purchased the log flume in 1970 and moved it to his newly renamed Goldrush Junction. This water ride continued to operate after the park became Silver Dollar City and Dollywood. The log flume remained at Dollywood until it became too old to maintain and was replaced with newer attractions. Even though the flume is gone, Dollywood will always have this direct connection to the history of World's Fairs.

The 1982 Knoxville World's Fair was considerably smaller than most of the other grand expositions throughout history. Perhaps the proliferation of theme parks around the globe destroyed the novelty of a World's Fair. Regardless, when you pass the Sunsphere, take a moment to realize that Dollywood may not exist at all without the history of World's Fairs.

SEVIERVILLE

As you drive from I-40 and toward the mountains, the first tourist town you will encounter is Sevierville. The seat of Sevier County and hometown of Dolly Parton, Sevierville is where the highway becomes Parkway. You will find many hotels and discover that Sevierville is home to the newer outlet malls.

I used to find Sevierville too far from Dollywood to choose as a place to stay. However, Veterans Boulevard has made getting to the park from Sevierville much quicker and the hotels tend to have a better price here. Expect it to take around twenty minutes to get to Dollywood from Sevierville with no traffic on Veterans Boulevard. On weekends and during Christmas, it can take double that.

Dolly fans will not want to miss Sevier County's tribute to its favorite daughter. A bronze statue of Dolly sits on the east lawn of the Sevier County Courthouse. It's not hard to find the courthouse. Just head to downtown Sevierville and look for the tall white bell-tower. The sculpture was cast by artist Jim Gray and depicts Dolly, barefoot, sitting on a large rock with her guitar. People claim that if you rub the statue, you will have good luck.

Dolly was often frustrated by her stoic father's lack of outward enthusiasm for her achievements. When the statue was dedicated, she remarked to her father that even he had to be impressed by it. Her dad admitted that to Dolly's fans the statue was impressive, but to pigeons it was just another outhouse! Years later, after his death, Dolly's mother told her that Mr. Parton went to the statue with a bucket of water every week to scrub it clean. Often, actions speak louder than words.

The official website of Sevierville is visitsevierville.com. There are a lot of websites masquerading as official and may not offer the best information. As a general rule, if a website is more concerned with selling you something than giving you free guidance, it's probably not maintained by the city.

SEVIERVILLE FACTS

Population:	14,807
Hotels on tripadvisor.com:	20
Restaurants on tripadvisor.com:	128
Elevation:	903 feet

Butterfly Wisdom

The Dolly statue is the area's tribute to Dolly. But, if you want to find Dolly's tribute to the area, you just need to listen for it in her music. Following are a few suggested songs that speak of Dolly's love for the Smoky Mountains. These titles are widely available in digital and audio form.

- "In My Tennessee Mountain Home" from My Tennessee Mountain Home, 1973
- "Heartsong" from Heartsongs: Live from Home, 1994
- "Paradise Road" from Hungry Again, 1998
- "Smoky Mountain Memories" from Live and Well, 2004 (This song appears on multiple albums; I like this version because Dolly tells the story of the song on the recording.)
- "My Mountains, My Home" from Sha-Kon-O-Hey, 2009

- "Forever Home" from Sha-Kon-O-Hey, 2009 (Actually, the entire Sha-Kon-O-Hey recording is a tribute to the Smoky Mountains. The songs were critically acclaimed as representing the best of Dolly's songwriting prowess.)
- "Home" from Blue Smoke, 2014

PIGEON FORGE

Parkway through Pigeon Forge is jam-packed with hotels, restaurants, shows, and attractions. There's a lot to do here and shopping could occupy more than one day alone. It's closer to Dollywood, though Parkway has notoriously bad traffic on weekends.

You will soon discover that Dolly Parton's Stampede and Dolly Parton's Pirate Adventure are not the only dinner shows in town. There are several to choose from in Pigeon Forge. Feuding families, comedians, and musicians are just a sample of the many theaters available. Basically, all these places offer a large dinner and show for one price. There are often some add-on items such as specialty drinks and photographs. Expect to pay around $40 per show. The best way to choose a dinner show is to ask another family staying at your hotel. Find some families around the pool with similar age children and ask if they enjoyed any of the shows in town. Since the food and show is different each year at these places, word-of-mouth is the best advertising they have. There used to be a number of show-only theaters on Parkway, but those have disappeared in recent years as families find it easier to go to just one place and pay an all-inclusive price.

I previously wrote that I was done talking about Dolly's properties, but then she went and bought another dinner show, although it's never advertised that she owns it. I've visited the Hatfield and McCoy Dinner Show several times and enjoyed it each time. I'm all about good customer service and this particular dinner show far exceeds in that regard. The Hatfields and McCoys may despise each other, but they love the audience equally—you will feel that. Once you are seated in their clean and well-designed theater, you will be served the best food of any dinner show in town. I'm absolutely addicted to Granny's Pulled Pork; I don't know if Granny is a Hatfield or a McCoy—and I really don't care—as long as she continues to serve the pork. The all-you-can-eat feast also included fried chicken, mashed potatoes, cole slaw, corn, vegetable soup, and a choice of chocolate or banana pudding. Here, the dinner is enjoyed before the show begins. It's quite a show with fantastic sets, costumes, and a bit of a story about the whole feud. There's a lot of live music, some great dancing, acrobatics—and an amazing segment of stunt diving that occurs in a real pool located under the stage! There is enough pottie humor to keep the kids interested, including an exploding outhouse, but this humor is not overdone and the show doesn't get annoying. Tickets are around $50 for adults and $25 for children; tickets are available at hatfieldmccoydinnerfeud.com.

Pigeon Forge has many restaurants without a show to choose from. Mostly, they are fast food and moderately priced establishments. There are not too many upscale dining choices here. Restaurants that cater to families can get quite busy during dinnertime, especially on weekends and all summer. To avoid a long wait, eat early or late. Outside practically every gift shop in town, you will find racks of area brochures and guidebooks. Pick up several of these as they are full of coupons. The restaurants have to compete a bit for your business and coupons are the way they do it.

If you're traveling from other parts of the United States you might be unaware of the restricted liquor laws that remain in some Southern counties. Technically, Sevier County is a dry county; it's not legal to buy or consume liquor in the county. However, noting the unique tourist culture of some parts of the county, each municipality within the county can create their own liquor ordinances. Gatlinburg has the most liberal policy and liquor can be both consumed in restaurants and purchased in stores. Sevierville serves liquor in restaurants only; you cannot purchase alcohol anywhere else. After two failed initiatives in 2009 and 2011, Pigeon Forge voters decided to allow liquor in 2013. Pigeon Forge restaurants can now serve liquor, and beer with no more than 6.2 percent alcohol is available at stores. Harder liquors and wine are available in Pigeon Forge, but only if they are produced in the county at a local winery or distillery.

The attractions on the tourist strip come in all sorts and varieties. You'll find family museum attractions that charge admission to look at interesting things that are famous and/or historical. There are plenty of go-cart courses in town that usually also offer miniature golf. Several arcades are located along with extreme rides that require bungee cords. You can even roll down a hill in a large inflatable ball. Whitewater rafting and zip lines are very popular. Even though these activities might occur in the mountains, the companies arranging them have shops on Parkway to take reservations.

Shopping is everywhere in Pigeon Forge. You'll notice the large outlet malls as you drive down Parkway. Just don't look past the small gift shops right off the road. These places sometimes look like they're one storm away from destruction, but they are fun to browse and have free parking. I'm not in the business of promoting particular stores because I think it's more fun for you to explore yourself. However, I really like the Incredible Christmas Place. You'll easily find it because it looks like a German Village. This huge shop sells every kind of Christmas thing you can imagine. But even if you're not looking to purchase anything, it's a fun place to browse because the atmosphere is well themed.

Speaking of Christmas, Pigeon Forge does an especially nice job of decorating for the holidays. The city's annual Winterfest begins on Veterans Day and lasts through February. The median running down the middle of Parkway is full of large light installations that have recently been fitted with bright LED bulbs. Not only is

Patriot Park full of lights, but it's also the place to board a heated trolley for a $5.00 tour of lights.

THE ISLAND

It may sound odd, due to the lack of an ocean or lake, but yes, there is a natural island in the middle of Pigeon Forge. The Little Pigeon River splits for just a bit, creating an island between the two streams. It's just enough room for an entertainment district—but not enough room for the parking lot. However, the parking lot is quite close (just across the stream), and here is the best part: there is no cost to park at The Island. There is also no admission charged!

The Island is a fairly new development, so everything is clean and well constructed. It's hard to miss because the tallest structure in town, the Great Smoky Mountain Wheel, is located on its property. As you approach, follow the signs to the parking lot that is across one segment of the Little Pigeon River. The parking lot is immense, and free trams are available to take you to The Island. But it's also nice to take a scenic walk across the small bridge.

The centerpiece of the development is a multitiered dancing fountain that is free to view. Lots of chairs surround the fountain that puts on a show every half hour from 10:00 a.m. to 11:30 p.m. Some of the fountain's nozzles shoot water more than sixty feet in the air, and everything is choreographed to music. At night, colorful lights make the show just a little better than during the day. Surrounding the fountain is a complex of shops and restaurants on the first floor, and Jimmy Buffet's Margaritaville Hotel is on the entire second floor.

The Margaritaville Hotel is the most expensive in Pigeon Forge—higher rates than at Dollywood's DreamMore Resort. In its defense, the hotel is extraordinary. Rooms have great views of the fountain show, the river, or the village shopping district. There is a rooftop pool, and all rooms have an outdoor balcony, something that is sorely lacking at Dollywood's flagship hotel. The Margaritaville Hotel features a restaurant and shop, both with a Caribbean theme.

There are several sit-down restaurants and quick-service snack bars on The Island. But the most remarkable is Paula Deen's Family Kitchen. Paula's always has quite a wait for a table—often two or three hours! But don't worry; they have an excellent system in place. Just call the restaurant about two hours before you want to dine. They will put your name on a list. When you arrive, check in at Paula's store underneath the dining room. The restaurant will send you a text when your table is ready, so you can explore the rest of The Island as you wait.

Meals at Paula Deen's Family Kitchen are served family-style. Each table selects its own entrees and sides. Everything is brought out on large serving platters. The chicken potpie is amazing and has ruined me for life—I can never eat someone else's potpie again. Biscuits and dessert are included. Needless to say, you must go hungry. Do not go to Paula Deen's Family Kitchen the same day as a visit to Dolly Parton's Stampede—you will not survive. Paula's store, underneath the restaurant, includes a kitchen for cooking demonstrations and all the butter-themed souvenirs you can imagine. If you don't have enough time to enjoy Paula Deen's Family Kitchen, you can get the same food quicker and cheaper at her fast outlet, The Bag Lady, located across the fountain from the restaurant.

The other food options take a wide range and include several more restaurants, an ice-cream shop, fudge store, bakeries, a fantastic pizzeria, hot-dog stand, and coffee shop. There is a very large candy store and equally large beef-jerky outlet.

The Great Smoky Mountain Wheel is a two-hundred-foot observation wheel of glass-enclosed capsules. The capsules are climate controlled and provide fantastic views of the Smoky Mountains. If you won't have a chance to get to Gatlinburg and the national park, then this wheel will be especially worth your time. The cost is $14 per adult for five rotations on the wheel. I'm very budget conscience, but each time I've been on the wheel, I've felt like I got my money's worth.

Next to the wheel are some small rides for kids and a very large arcade. The arcade is diverse and has a few games I've not seen anywhere else. You can win tickets that are stored on a card and can be redeemed for the typical prizes. Kids (and lots of adults) will also enjoy other activities available on The Island: a ropes course, mirror maze, dark-ride adventure, escape room, old-time photo, a miniature train called The Island Express, bungee trampoline, carousel, and shooting gallery.

The Island is home to Alcatraz East Crime Museum. You won't be able to miss this large prison-like structure. The museum includes exhibits on crime and crime fighting in the United States. There is a large area dedicated to forensics and fans of *CSI* will find this portion fascinating. Alcatraz East also displays John Dillinger's Car and Al Capone's Rosary (the rosary looks new, I don't think it was used all that much).

There are plenty of shops (around 60 of them) on The Island, many of which are unique to the Smoky Mountains. The shops sell a large variety of merchandise including: home décor, Christmas items, toys, kitchen goods, sporting goods, nature products, and nostalgic gifts. The Island also contains a moonshine distillery and micro brewpub. Both of these establishments offer live music.

Just like everyplace else in the Smokies, The Island goes all out for the holidays. The fountain show takes on a Christmas theme and there are decorations galore, including an enormous tree. The Island is the place to be on New Year's Eve.

Before you depart for The Island, make sure to check out islandinpigeonforge.com. The bottom of their website contains a link for coupons, and you will find that many of the property's establishments have good deals to print. Their motto is: eat, shop, play, and stay; and they deliver these activities in a clean and safe environment. The complex is a welcome addition to the Pigeon

Forge tourist strip. With something to do for everyone, The Island is worth your time and vacation dollars.

Pigeon Forge loves to number its traffic lights along Parkway. You'll see these numbers above each intersection. While you look at billboards and ads in magazines, the different establishments will state which traffic light they're located near. For example, The Island is located off light #7. Parkway begins with traffic light #0 near Sevierville and continues to light #10 on the way to Gatlinburg. This doesn't mean that there's just ten traffic lights. As new attractions and streets are added, new lights are given a letter after their number. So, you might find yourself looking for light #2B. For reference, Dollywood Lane is traffic light #8.

The official website of Pigeon Forge is mypigeonforge.com.

PIGEON FORGE FACTS

Population:	6,199
Hotels on tripadvisor.com:	92
Restaurants on tripadvisor.com:	120
Elevation:	1,001 feet

GATLINBURG

At the very base of the mountains and next to the entrance to the national park, you'll find the small hamlet of Gatlinburg. You'll also find New York City traffic. To be fair, that's not quite true. The traffic in New York is actually better.

Please know that I'm not telling you this to stop you from going. On the contrary, no visit to the area is complete without seeing Gatlinburg. However, I want you to be prepared enough to plan your visit.

You will want to park and walk in compact Gatlinburg. Unless you have a hotel on the Gatlinburg strip, you will pay for parking. There are several municipal lots and some privately owned parking places. Each will have their price displayed as you enter. Expect to pay $10–$15 for a day of parking. The closer you get to the center of town, the less walking you will have to do, but it will be more expensive to park. Gatlinburg operates its own trolley system, very similar to the Pigeon Forge trolleys. In fact, the two systems connect at the Gatlinburg Visitor's Center as you come into town.

Gatlinburg has as many shops and restaurants as Pigeon Forge, but everything is much closer to each other. Also, Gatlinburg offers a few more upscale dining options than its cousins up the road.

There are no dinner shows here, but there are plenty of evening attractions to keep the family occupied. An endless number of arcades, fun houses, and assorted weird museums line the strip. There's also miniature golf, an observation tower, and a ski lift to the top of a nearby mountain. I particularly enjoy the quiet ride up the ski lift to get a great view of the mountains, especially if the weather is clear.

Smoky Mountain Tunes and Tales is a festival that offers street performances through spring and summer. During weekends in spring, and every night in summer, folk musicians and storytellers perform at various locations along the tourist strip. Since there is no admission to get into the city, all these performances are free! During Christmas, Winter Magic Tunes and Tales is presented. The musicians and storytellers change their acts to focus on songs and stories of the holidays. Gatlinburg does an especially nice job of decorating their tourist strip for Christmas. Large decorative trees with thousands of white lights line the street and make it feel like you are driving through a snowy lane.

Perhaps the most famous event in Gatlinburg is the annual Nation's First Fourth of July Parade. The parade begins at midnight on July 4 (the night of July 3). Traveling down the strip through the center of town, the parade is followed by fireworks.

The most unique experience in town is the Gatlinburg Arts and Crafts Community Loop. This is actually the nation's largest organization of independent artists and crafters. The loop will take you eight miles into the hills. Along the way, stop and visit the shops of handmade goods galore. Quilts, candles, baskets, metalwork, leather, jewelry, musical instruments, dolls, toys, and ceramics are among the many offerings. Make sure you grab the Gatlinburg Arts and Crafts Guide before you begin the loop. The guide is widely available at hotels and restaurants on the strip; it will provide a map and list of crafters. If you decide not to drive yourself, a dedicated trolley continuously makes the loop with frequent stops near the shops. The trolley costs $1.

The official website for Gatlinburg is gatlinburg.com. You can download the Gatlinburg Arts and Crafts Guide from the site as well as a map of parking options.

GATLINBURG FACTS

Population:	4,206
Hotels on tripadvisor.com:	78
Restaurants on tripadvisor.com:	119
Elevation:	1,289 feet

Butterfly Wisdom

If you've experienced the entire drive from I-40 through the three towns and into the national park, you've seen lots of chain restaurants, local establishments, dinner shows, diners, and steak places. You've also surely noticed the abundance of pancake houses. Breakfast has become a ritual in the Smokies and the pancake house is almost as traditional as the dulcimer. Whether themed like a log cabin or covered wagon, these restaurants all serve stacks of pancakes with fresh maple syrup.

The pancake houses are, of course, always open for breakfast. A few remain open and offer lunch; they normally close in the afternoon. In addition to pancakes, most houses serve a complete menu of breakfast items including eggs, sausage, waffles, and bacon. You will almost always find coupons for these places in the free brochures outside many tourist shops. Even if you get a free breakfast at your hotel, it can be a nice treat for your family to enjoy a leisurely morning at a pancake house.

They are so numerous that it would take months to do a review of each establishment. I've dined at many and you will find that they are all quite similar. However, if you enjoy the very thick and hearty style of true pan "cakes," then head to Crockett's Breakfast Camp on the mountain end of the Gatlinburg strip.

GREAT SMOKY MOUNTAINS NATIONAL PARK

And now for the reason any of this is here in the first place. Would there even be a Dolly Parton without the mountains that inspired her? If you've never seen them before, your first glimpse of the Smokies in the distance won't seem like much. But suddenly, you are close enough to see the steam rising all over and your jaw will drop.

You thought you were looking at a normal cloud in the sky. But as you get closer you see that it's actually an entire mountain floating in smoke before you. It takes your mind a moment to change perception while you realize that the sky is not the sky. Soon, you will be close enough to see not just one, but hundreds of smoking mountains. Your perception will continue to change the farther you drive into the park.

Incredibly beautiful and unique, the vegetation on the mountains is so dense that moisture is trapped everywhere. As the sun heats various surfaces, even in winter, the moisture turns to steam and rises to the heavens. Nowhere else on Earth does this same situation exist. It's the perfect combination of topography, climate, and vegetation.

Geologists believe that the Smoky Mountains escaped the glaciers from the last few ice ages. This lack of destruction allowed many types of plants to remain that had been destroyed elsewhere. There are more different types of flora and fauna inside the park than at any other location in the United States—including Hawaii! Joining the plants are 21,000 living species including 67 mammal types, 80 groups of reptiles, 67 types of fish, 2,000 species of birds, and over 17,000 different families of insects. The park is known as the "Salamander Capital of the World" as 34 species of salamander can be found here.

The Cherokee Indians, a branch of the Iroquois Nation, can trace their ancestors in the Smokies back over one-thousand years. Of course, the mountains weren't called the Smokies then. The Cherokee called them Shaconage, pronounced sha-kon-o-hey, which means "land of blue smoke."

You can explore more than 800 miles of hiking trails. Even if it's hot and humid in Dollywood, there has never been a temperature over eighty-degrees recorded on top of Mount LeConte—never! The park totals more than 520,000 acres and is designated an International Biosphere Reserve.

There are many guidebooks written about Great Smoky Mountains National Park. After all, it's the most visited national park in the United States. The books are available online, or at the Sugarlands Visitor Center. As you enter the park from the Gatlinburg strip, the Sugarlands Visitor Center is clearly labeled. The center offers a museum, clean restrooms, bookstore, and information desk. Rangers are available to answer any question you have. Since other authors know a lot more about the mountains than I do, I'll let you get one of their books. I'll just write about a few of my favorite places here.

My favorite picnic place is called Chimney Tops. It's easy to find off the main road and is clearly labeled. I like this spot because each picnic table includes its own parking spot and grill. This scenic place is nestled against the West Prong Little Pigeon River and there are always people sitting on rocks and dipping into the cool fresh water. Heavily shaded by trees, you won't have to worry about getting too much sun here. Restrooms and garbage facilities are nearby. Always leave your picnic spot cleaner than you found it. I like to believe there is a special place in hell for those who leave trash in national parks.

Newfound Gap is right on the Tennessee/North Carolina border. There is a large parking area to take in the beautiful scenery. The Appalachian Trail runs through this area and you may see thru-hikers on their 2,160-mile journey. There are several great photo opportunities from this place, of course most include the spectacular mountains. However, a fun photo is to stand on the border between the two states that are marked with a sign.

A bit higher than Newfound Gap, Clingmans Dome is the tallest mountain of the Smokies and the highest point in Tennessee. It's also the highest point of the Appalachian Trail at 6,643 feet. At the top is a 45-foot observation tower that's just high enough to see over the trees. As you can imagine, the view is amazing! The tower is free and accessible to everyone by a spiral ramp. The road to Clingmans Dome is closed in the winter.

You could read books for days about Great Smoky Mountains National Park, and I hope you do because it's that special. However prepared you are for whatever you want to do, just remember that it's nature and safety is important. Pay attention to all park guidelines and regulations. Even though it's literally what you're doing, hiking is more than just a walk in the park. Be prepared, stay hydrated, and always have some way to communicate.

2020 DOLLYWOOD AND BEYOND!

GREAT SMOKY MOUNTAINS NATIONAL PARK FACTS

Area:	522,419 acres
Visitors in 2018:	11,421,200
Campgrounds:	10 (total of 1,000 spaces)
Picnic Areas:	11 (total of 1,050 tables)
Streams:	2,115 miles
Trails:	800 miles
Lowest Elevation:	840 feet
Highest Elevation:	6,643 feet

MOST VISITED NATIONAL PARKS (2018)

1. Great Smoky Mountains	11,421,200
2. Grand Canyon	6,380,495
3. Rocky Mountain	4,590,493
4. Zion	4,320,033
5. Yellowstone	4,115,000
6. Yosemite	4,009,436
7. Acadia	3,537,575
8. Grand Teton	3,491,151
9. Olympic	3,104,455
10. Glacier	2,965,309

"There are trees here that stood before our forefathers ever came to this continent; there are brooks that still run as clear as on the day the first pioneer cupped his hand and drank from them. In this park, we shall conserve these trees, the pine, the red-bud, the dogwood, the azalea, the rhododendron, the trout and the thrush bird for the happiness of the American people."

—Franklin D. Roosevelt at the dedication of Great Smoky Mountains National Park

The beauty of the trees, the softness of the air,
The fragrance of the grass, speaks to me.
The summit of the mountain, the thunder of the sky,
The rhythm of the stream, speaks to me.
The fairness of the stars, the freshness of the morning,
The dew drop on the flower, speaks to me.
The strength of the fire, the taste of the fish,
The trail of the sun, and the life that never goes away,
They speak to me.
And my heart soars.

—Cherokee poem by an unknown person about Shaconage (Land of Blue Smoke)

TIME TO GO...

I hope you've enjoyed reading this guide as much as I enjoyed writing it. This has truly been a labor of love...love for theme parks, love for Dollywood, and love for the memories I have. I wish you those same wonderful memories. In the great theme park of life, I hope you spend a lot more time on the rides than you do waiting in line.

Now it's time to stop reading and start traveling! And, as Dolly Parton tells her audience at the end of every live show, if you liked it...tell someone about it. If you didn't like it, then keep your mouth closed.

Hooray for Dollywood!

2020 DOLLYWOOD AND BEYOND!

MAP 1: SMOKY MOUNTAIN TOURIST REGION

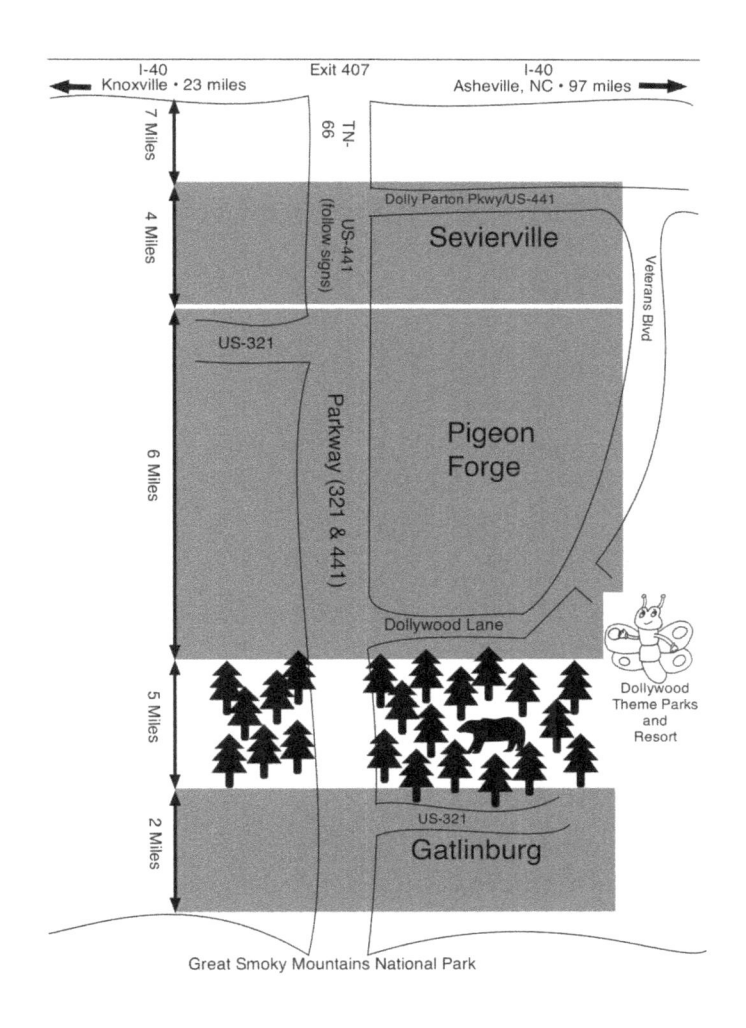

MAP 2: ARRIVING AT DOLLYWOOD

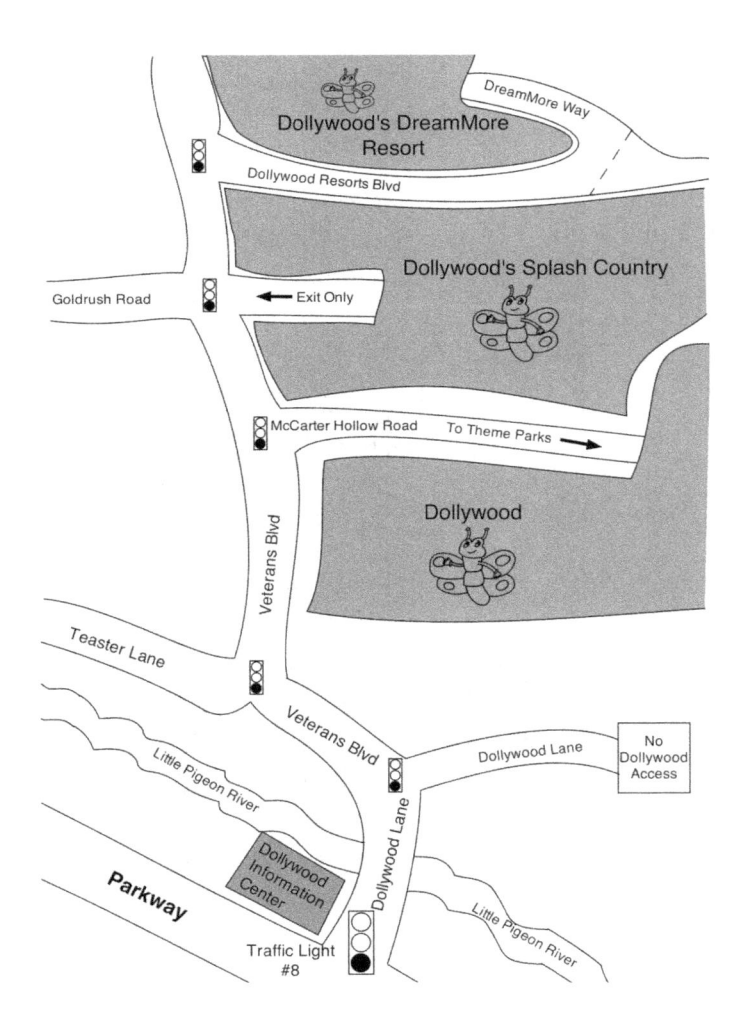

2020 DOLLYWOOD AND BEYOND!

MAP 3: DOLLYWOOD PARKING LOTS

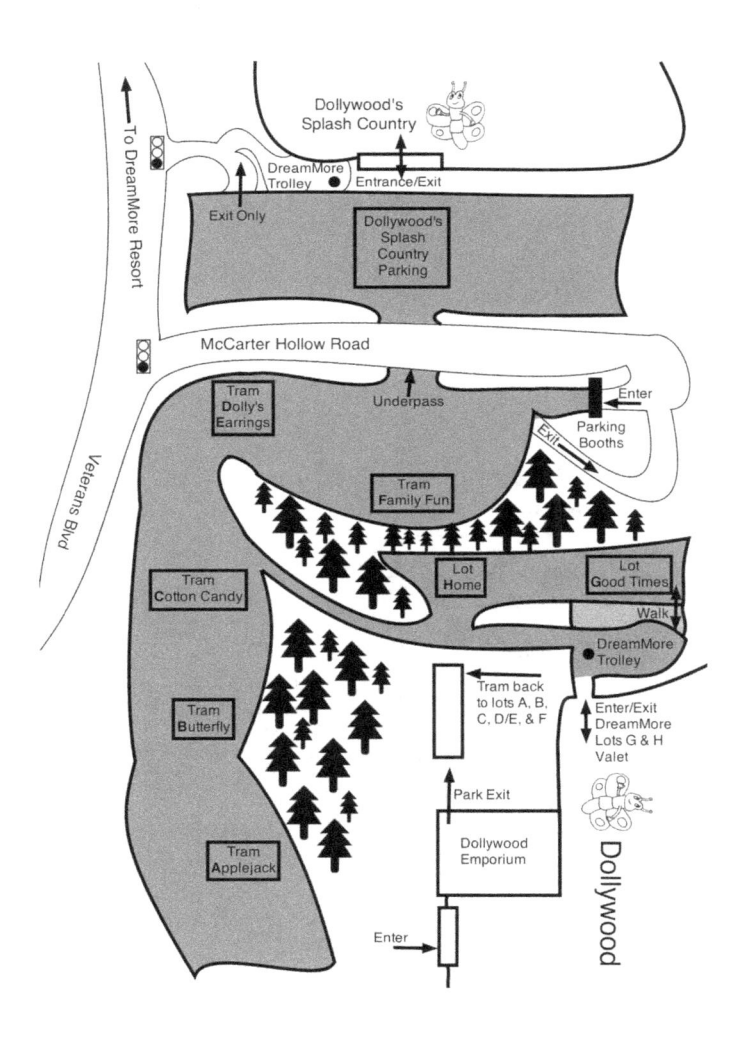

MAP 4: DOLLYWOOD LANDS

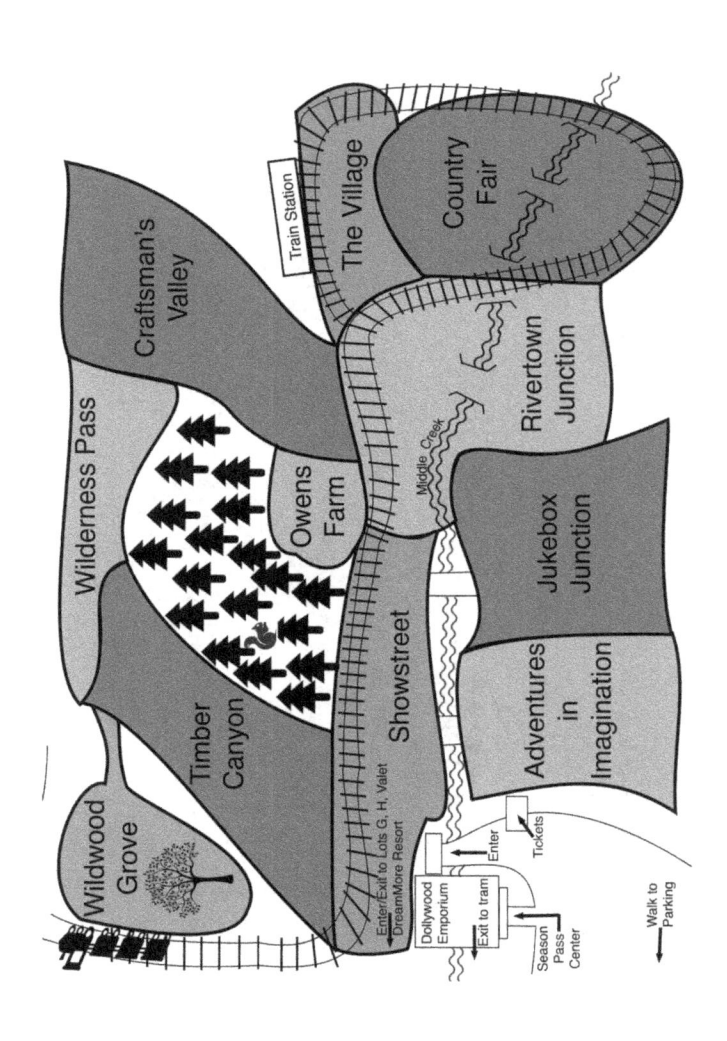

INDEX

Adventures in Imagination 98-103
Amazing Flying Elephants 120
Anderson, Jada Star (see Jada Star)
Appalachian Trail 226
Aunt Granny's Buffet 114
Autry, Gene 17
Awards 23-25

Back Porch Theater 117
Bakery 87
Barbeque and Bluegrass 194
Barnstormer 131
Barry J. 137, 145
Bathhouses 175
Beat Mountain Fire Tower 180
Beaver Tails, 187
Berries and Cream 187
Big Bear Plunge 180
Black Bear Trail 158
Blazing Fury 147
Blue Ribbon Pavilion 123-124
Busy Bees 121
Butterfly Waterslide 185

Calico Falls Schoolhouse 146
Camp DW 51

Campsite Grill 188
Canopy 177-178
Cascades, The 186
Cascades Concessions 188
Celebration Hall 123-124
Centralized Measuring 83, 175
Chapel 139
Chasing Rainbows Museum 101-103
Cherokee (Indigenous People) 16, 225, 228
Chimney Tops 225-226
Christmas in the Smokies Show 94-95
Christmas Songbook Show 145
Clingman's Dome 226
Cinnamon Bread 133-134
Costner and Sons Magic Shop 127
Country Cookers 111
Country Crossroads Show 137
Country Fair 119-124
Craftsman's Valley 133-148
Crockett's Breakfast Camp 224
Custom Glassworks 138
Cyrus, Miley 102

DM Pantry 46
DP's Celebrity Theater 94-95
Daredevil Falls 142
Demolition Derby 121
Disney, Walt 18, 21, 68
Dixie Stampede (see Dolly Parton's Stampede)
Dizzy Disc 122
Doggywood 78
Doghouse 153
Dogs N Taters 118-119, 188
Dolly Dollars 83

Dolly Parton (see Parton, Dolly)
Dolly Parton's Stampede 90, 207-210
Dolly's Closet Shop 100
Dolly's Home on Wheels 101
Dolly's Tennessee Mountain Home 115-116
Dollywood App 106
Dollywood Boulevard 98-99
Dollywood Emporium 82-83
Dollywood Express 128-130
Dollywood's Smoky Mountain Cabins 56
Downbound Float Trip 180-181
Dragonflier 161
Dreamland Drive-In Show 104
Dreammore Resort 22, 40-55
Dreammore Resort, Christmas at 53-54
Dreammore Salon and Spa 51-52
Dreamsong Theater 99-100
Dropline 166-167

Eagle Mountain Sanctuary 143-144
Eagle's Flight Outfitters 150
Eagle's Nest Shop 144

Festival of Nations 192-193
Fire Tower Falls 181
FireChaser Express 152-153
Firehouse Fun Yard 151-152
Fireworks 195-196
Flashbulb Photos 86
Flower and Food Festival 193-194
Frogs & Fireflies 159
Front Porch Cafe 90

Gatlinburg 32, 57-58, 191, 221-223

MICHAEL FRIDGEN

Gem Tones 106
Gingerbread Recipe 205-206
Gold Pass 61
Goldrush Junction 19-20
Gospel Hall of Fame 86
Grab and Go 188
Grandstand Cafe 122
Granny Ogle's Ham and Beans 137-138
Granny Owens Toys 132
Granny's Garden 130
Great Pumpkin LumiNights 37, 199-200
Great Smoky Mountain National Park 16-17, 26-29, 67, 224-228
Great Tree Swing 157
Grist Mill 133-134

Harvest Festival 197-198
Hatfields and McCoys Dinner Show 215-216
Heartsong Theater 126-127
Herschend Family Entertainment 70
Herschend, Hugo 19
Herschend, Jack 19-20
Herschend, Mary 19
Herschend, Peter 19-20
Hickory House Bar-b-q 143
Hidden Hollow 160
High Country Provisions 188
Hillside General Store 140
Holly Jolly Junction 141-142
Hurricane Hazel 16-18

Imagination Library Playhouse 127
Island, The 218-221
It's a Wonderful Life Show 85-86

J., Barry (see Barry J.)
Jada Star 100, 137, 145
Jukebox Junction 103-110

Kaman's Art Shoppes 145
Knoxville 33, 212-213
Knoxville Airport (see Tyson McGhee Airport)
Knoxville World's Fair 212-213

Lazy River 180-181
Lemon Twist 121
Lightning Rod 107-109
Lil' Pilots Playground 131
Little Creek Falls 181
Lucky Ducky 120
Lucky Seven Mine & Gem Shop 146
Lumber Jack's Pizza 165-166
Lumberjack Lifts 165

Mad Mockingbird 160
Market Square 110
Midway Market 122-123
Mine Shaft, The 163
Miss Lillian's Bar-b-q Corner 136
Miss Lillian's Chicken House 136
Miss Mamie's Pizza 189
Miss Sally's Sit-n-Sip 134
Modell, Art 19-20
Mountain Blown Glass Factory 115
Mountain Grove Merchants 158
Mountain Laurel Home Shop 113-114
Mountain Scream 182
Mountain Twist 182
Mountain Waves 182

Mountain Waves Hydration Station 189
My People Show 99-100
Mystery Mine 162-163

Newfound Gap 226

O Holy Night Show 137
Ogle, Judy 104, 138
Old Flames Candles 140-141
Old Time Flashbulb Photos 125
Opryland 10, 20
Outpost Snacks 189
Owens Farm 130-132

Pancake Houses 223-224
PaPaw's Roadside Country Market 124-125
Parton, Cassie 99
Parton, Dolly 20-21, 28, 68-73, 98-103, 115-116, 126-127, 141, 163-164, 213-215
Parton, Heidi Lou 100
Parton, Randy 99
Pig Pen 131
Pigeon Forge 10, 19, 31-32, 57-58, 191, 215-218
Pigeon Forge Trolley 35-36
Piggy Parade 120
Pines Theater 104-105
Pirate's Voyage Dinner Show 90, 211
Plaza at Wilderness Pass 154-155
Pokeberry Lane Shop 47

Racing River Rapids 183
Rebel Railroad 19
Red's Drive-In Restaurant 105
Refillable Mug 111, 186-187

Retreats 177-179
Ride Accessibility Center 83
RiverRush 183-184
Riverside Trading Post 189-190
Rivertown Junction 110-119
Rivertown Trading 118
Robbins, Grover 18-19
Rockin' Roadway 109
Roosevelt, Franklin Delano 16, 227
Rudolph, the Red-Nosed Reindeer 17, 141-142

Santa's Workshop 123-124
Schoolhouse 146
Scrambler 120
Season Pass 60-65
Sevierville 32, 57-58, 191, 213-214
Shooting Star 121
Showstreet 81-98
Showstreet Palace Theater 85-86
Showstreet Snacks 90
Silver Dollar City 19-20
Sky Rider 122
Skyview Snacks 151
Slick Rock Racer 184
Smoking 88-89
Smoky Creek Leather 134
Smoky Mountain Christmas 37, 66, 85-86, 94-95, 104-105, 123-124, 137, 144-145, 155, 160, 200-205
Smoky Mountain Christmas Cottage 115
Smoky Mountain River Rampage 112
Song & Hearth Restaurant 45-46
Songbook Show 137
Southern Gospel Music Association 86
Southern Life Shop 95-96

Southern Pantry, The 89-90
Splash and Dash Sundries 190
Splinter's Snacks 153
Spotlight Bakery 87
Stone, Kevin 151
Stone-Penland Pottery 138-139
Summer Celebration 194-196
Sunny Munny 177
Sunscreen 174
Super Pass 62
Super Gold Pass 62
Sweet Shoppe 87-88
Sweets and Treats 157
Swiftwater Run 184

Tailspin Racer 185
Taste Traders 140
Temple's Mercantile 125-126
Tennessee Tornado 148
Thunderhead Coaster 167-168
Tickets 46-47, 58-65
Till & Harvest 156-157
Timber Canyon 162-169
Timesaver 91-93, 176-177
Tin Sign Shoppe 118
Train (see Dollywood Express)
Treetop Tower 157
'Twas the Night Before Christmas Show 104-105
Tweetsie Railroad 18-19
Tyson McGhee Airport 33-34

VIP Tour 132
Valley Exhibition Center 141-142
Valley Forge Blacksmith 142-143

Valley Theater 137
Valley Wood Carvers 139-140
Victoria's Pizza 125
Village, The 124-130
Village Carousel 126
Volunteer Supply Company 154

Walzing Swinger 122
Water Hole, The 189
Weather 38-39
Whistle Punk Chaser 167
Wild Eagle 149-150
Wild River Falls 186
Wilderness Pass 149-155
Wildwood Creek 158
Wildwood Grove 156-161
Wildwood Tree, The 159-160
Wings of America Theater 144-145
World's Fair 212-213

CPSIA information can be obtained
at www.ICGtesting.com
Printed in the USA
BVHW040203180621
609844BV00014BA/533